HORIZON

AUTUMN, 1964 · VOLUME VI, NUMBER 4

Our Loyal Opposition

Since the first issue appeared in 1958, HORIZON has attracted a considerable amount of critical comment, most of it highly favorable. We have found a large and interested audience, which we hope to increase as the seasons pass. Occasionally the influence of what we have published has been felt far beyond our circle of subscribers through reprints of articles that have excited special interest. Most recently, for example, Morroe Berger's "The Black Muslims" (in the Winter 1964 issue, the first of our quarterly numbers) was not only picked up by the Japanese magazine *Jiya*, but was widely distributed among the "intellectuals and university faculty" in Pakistan by the United States Information Agency.

Another acknowledgment and note of appreciation from the East comes in a letter from a young Siamese student who had chanced upon the same Winter issue in his college library, and discovered in it Archie Robertson's article "The King and Us." His letter to us concludes: "You are a marvelous ambassador for your country in trying to combine firmly the relationship between our nations. . . . On behalf of my country and the Siamese people, please receive the thankfulness from our nation which has been your good friend—as you say—and will be your friend indeed perpetually as you are to us now."

The most immediate source of satisfaction to the editors of HORIZON is in such unsolicited letters from our subscribers and others who have thoughtfully expressed their opinions of our efforts. To editor and publisher alike it would be a source of even greater satisfaction to meet and talk with all the subscribers on our list, but this would involve a lifetime of engagements and it assumes an equal interest on the part of our readers. However, a few of us recently have in fact enjoyed the opportunity of interviewing personally a representative group of subscribers from various walks of life. HORIZON subscribers represent a wide spectrum of personal and professional interests. Housewives, lawyers, engineers, teachers, secretaries, and doctors are among those who read what we print, as well as actors, artists, musicians, writers, and publishers—and we welcome having a piece of their mind, so to speak. Virtually all those we talked with did indeed reciprocate our interest and were generous with both their time and opinions. Thanks to these pleasant dialogues and the letters we receive, we feel better able to realize our purposes, and we have a better understanding of both our merits and our shortcomings.

Among other things, we learn from such evidence that, like some other established institutions, HORIZON has developed a loyal opposition, whose constituents would change some things if they were sitting in our chair. To summarize these differences of opinion requires more space than is available at this point. One apparent division of interest is between those who would have us include more contemporary material

HORIZON is published every three months by American Heritage Publishing Co., Inc.

PRESIDENT
James Parton

EDITOR-IN-CHIEF
Joseph J. Thorndike

EDITORIAL DIRECTOR, HORIZON
Oliver Jensen

EDITORIAL DIRECTOR, BOOK DIVISION
Richard M. Ketchum

ART DIRECTOR
Irwin Glusker

Editorial and executive offices: 551 Fifth Avenue, New York, N.Y. 10017.

EDITOR
Marshall B. Davidson

MANAGING EDITOR: Ralph Backlund   ASSOCIATE EDITOR: Jane Wilson
ART DIRECTOR: Elton Robinson
ASSISTANT EDITORS: Shirley Abbott, Charles L. Mee, Jr., Mary Cable, Barbara Klaw EDITORIAL ASSISTANTS: Wendy Buehr, Priscilla Flood
LIBRARIAN: Caroline Backlund
COPY EDITOR: Mary Ann Pfeiffer *Assistant*: Joan Rehe

ADVISORY BOARD: Gilbert Highet, *Chairman*, Frederick Burkhardt, William Harlan Hale, Jotham Johnson, John Walker
EUROPEAN CONSULTING EDITOR: J. H. Plumb, *Christ's College, Cambridge*
EUROPEAN BUREAU: Gertrudis Feliu, *Chief, 11 rue du Bouloi, Paris I*

HORIZON

A Magazine of the Arts

AUTUMN, 1964 · VOLUME VI, NUMBER 4

and those who would prefer to see less of it than we run in our pages. Since the make-up of each issue varies somewhat from the next, our "opposition" on this point must fluctuate accordingly.

But this question of balance naturally remains a constant concern of the editors. HORIZON must and will keep its eye on the contemporary scene around the world. We may even aspire to be prophetic, in a sense, by attempting to recognize what is most valid and viable in the cultural developments of our own time—without losing a sense of humor in the attempt. However, we will by the same token look the more eagerly to the history of other ages for correctives to that "parochialism in time" which Bertrand Russell has termed one of the besetting faults of our modern society; a parochialism that in any progressive age tends to use the present as an absolute standard by which to evaluate the past. Thus, for instance, the Renaissance was blind to the Gothic art of earlier centuries and the seventeenth and eighteenth centuries whitewashed over priceless mosaics of a more remote past. And thus, also, Thucydides claimed that nothing of great importance had happened before his time. In his ignorance of the farther past, as Herbert Muller has observed, he could not realize the unique glory of Athens as well as we can today. It seems reasonable to conclude that the greater our awareness of the past the better we can realize the unique character of our contemporary civilization.

THE EDITORS

All correspondence about subscriptions should be addressed to: HORIZON Subscription Office, 379 West Center St., Marion, Ohio 43301.

Single Copies: $5.00
Subscriptions: $16.00 per year in the U.S. & Canada; elsewhere, $17.00

Annual indexes for Volumes I–V are available at $1 each. A cumulative index for Volumes I–V is available at $3. HORIZON is also indexed in the *Readers Guide to Periodical Literature*.

The editors welcome contributions but can assume no responsibility for unsolicited material.

Title registered U.S. Patent Office

Second-class postage paid at New York, N.Y., and at additional mailing offices.

COVER: The Presidential Bodyguard, led here by their sergeant-major, is the elite corps of the Indian Army. The history of the native corps, formed in 1773 to protect the British Governor General, provides a curious microcosm of the history of British rule in India. Originally set at one hundred cavalry, it was increased in 1803 to four hundred troops, two light guns, and a band. Throughout the nineteenth century, as British fortunes rose and fell, the numbers of the "bescarleted and silvered" corps rose and fell, too. Today, as India's Presidential Bodyguard, it is made up of three hundred men. The photograph is by Brian Brake, whose color portfolio of India today follows an article on Rudyard Kipling that begins on page 60.

Fragments of antique sculpture adorn a wall at the Villa Albani near Rome—"remnants of history which have casually escaped the shipwreck of time"

In earlier times pagan temples were converted into Christian churches, mausoleums made to serve as fortresses, sarcophagi put to use as bathtubs—by such thrifty and practical expedients untold treasures from classical antiquity have been preserved from ruin and destruction

Re-uses of the Past

By JOTHAM JOHNSON

The observant traveler in the Mediterranean, viewing the desolation of the Roman Forum or the Athenian Agora, may wonder why, of all the architectural splendor which once adorned these centers, there is so little to see. Why have so many buildings vanished entirely or survived only as broken walls? What happened to them? And if, wondering, he asks his guide, he will get only fragments of the truth. He may be told that the ancient temples and palaces were toppled by barbarian hordes; or that Christian zealots broke up the statues and tore down the temples which stood for paganism; or that the marble slabs and columns were burned in kilns to make lime for the mortar of later buildings; or that parts of the ancient structures still stand beneath the debris of centuries.

All these explanations contain some truth, but the scale of destruction is too great to be accounted for by any one of them. The key to the terrible attrition of the ancient buildings lies in the simple fact that people, by and large, are thrifty: they don't like throwing things away, and are pleased, even in times of prosperity, to find a new use for something old.

Of course, there have been many times in history when making do was an out-and-out necessity. During long periods when Greece and Italy endured intense and grinding poverty, when trade had all but ceased, when the mines and quarries and mills were silent, and when, in order to raise grain for the starving poor of the cities, country people were bound to their farms, the splendid temples and office buildings and ornaments of past generations represented a source of fat with which to satisfy the needs of the present.

Throughout the Dark Ages, when production of new metal was low, scrap bronze and iron assumed greater value. Bronze statues of bygone heroes were smashed with sledge hammers and tossed into the crucible. So were the warped and twisted bronze doors and grilles of buildings destroyed or damaged by fire. The clamps and dowels that gripped the stones of wall courses were painstakingly dug out not only for the bronze and iron of the clamps themselves but for the bits of lead with which they were soldered into place. And if obtaining these morsels meant tearing down a whole building, there were many uses for the dismantled building-stones.

In view of the continual demand for metal the occasional survival of works of sculpture in bronze—such as the Capitoline Wolf, the Chimera, the Serpent Column from Delphi in the Hippodrome at Constantinople, and the magnificent group of four

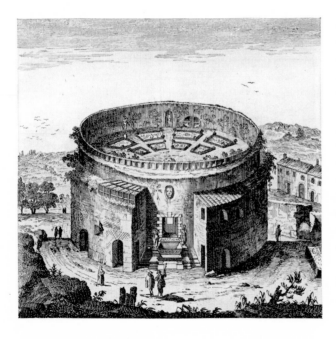

ABOVE: Campo Vaccino—*Cow Pasture*—is the title of this 16th-century view of the Roman Forum by the Dutch painter Wilhelm Neulandt. For more than a millennium the Forum was plundered and neglected. In 1536 some of the debris was cleared away for a celebration, after which the cows and cowherds moved in. They seem to have done little harm, for all the monuments Neulandt saw are still standing. The wine vendors at left set up shop in vaults near Palatine Hill. In the center are three columns of the Temple of Castor and Pollux, and beyond them the Basilica of Maxentius.

LEFT: *This 16th-century print shows how the grandiose mausoleum of Augustus was once pleasantly transformed into a garden.*

6

Byzantine horses which stand on the balcony of St. Mark's in Venice—may be regarded as a welcome happenstance. Luckily, there was always someone to whom these bronzes were more valuable as works of art than as junk.

The equestrian statue of the pagan emperor Marcus Aurelius, which stands triumphant in the Piazza del Campidoglio at Rome, owes its preservation to mistaken identity. It was spared because the Roman populace of the Middle Ages believed it to represent Constantine the Great, the first Christian emperor. The Delphi Charioteer (sole survivor of a bronze group that consisted of a four-horse chariot and a victorious racing prince and his groom), the Etruscan Orator from Chiusi, the famous Boxer in the Museo delle Terme, and a few others owe their survival to the luck of having been buried and forgotten before the need for metal became desperate. At Pompeii and Herculaneum volcanic ash and mud have preserved a few samples in bronze of the taste of the provincial first-century bourgeoisie. But some of the finest bronzes from ancient Greece—the Zeus from Cape Artemisium, the Marathon Boy, the Apollo Piombino, and the Demeter from Bodrum—have come from the floor of the Mediterranean, where, in Roman times, they sank with the vessels which were carrying them to Italy. It is one paradox of history that eighty feet of sea water has proved a more reliable preserver of bronzes than the most Grecophile Roman collector.

Not all the metal which lay ready to hand was melted down for scrap. If it could be salvaged intact, it might be re-used elsewhere. The frequency and the ingenuity of these re-uses have made Rome, especially, a vast puzzle in detection for the archaeologist bent on finding out what became of ancient bronzes. The emperor Honorius took the bronze roof tiles of the Basilica of Constantine, in the Roman Forum, for the first church of St. Peter. The Byzantine emperor Constans II, in the seventh century, ordered the gilded bronze roof tiles of the Pantheon taken down and shipped to Constantinople. About a thousand years later, in the seventeenth century, the Barberini pope, Urban VIII, sanctioned the removal of numerous bronze pieces from the roof of the Pantheon's portico. Some of the metal was used for cannon for the Castel Sant' Angelo, and the rest was given to Bernini to use for the four gilded spiral columns of the *baldacchino* of St. Peter's (*"Quod non fecerunt barbari, fecerunt Barberini,"* said a wag —"What the barbarians failed to do, the Barberini did"). The Pantheon and the Temple of the Divine Romulus still have their original bronze doors, which growl convincingly as they turn on the old pivots, but the bronze doors of the Curia Julia, the senate house of ancient Rome, were removed by Pope Alexander VII and installed in the main entrance of St. John Lateran, where they are today.

If the re-use of bronzes offers a historical puzzle, the fate of ancient marbles is even more of a challenge to the archaeological detective. Broken sculptures that escaped being burned for lime sometimes found a more bizarre destiny. At Rome, in the church of Sant' Agnese fuori le Mura, is a Roman statue converted by the sculptor Nicolas Cordier in 1600 into a figure of Saint Agnes. In the other Roman church of Saint Agnes, in the Piazza Navona, a Roman statue has been reworked as Saint Sebastian. In the crypt of St. Peter's is an ancient statue that has been restored to represent Saint Peter himself, and in Santa Croce in Gerusalemme the body of a marble Juno has been given a new head and renamed Saint Helena (see page 12). Embedded in the Arch of Constantine at Rome are relief panels and medallions which Constantine thriftily removed from older monuments to embellish his own arch; in at least two of these, portrait heads have been reworked in the likeness of Constantine.

Piranesi's Views of Rome *show many pagan structures reclaimed by the practical Christian clergy. This is the temple of Antoninus and Faustina in 1759, made over as a church.*

In the thirties, while I was directing excavations for the University of Pennsylvania Museum at the Roman colony of Minturnae, on the Appian Way between Rome and Naples, we found in the wreckage of the theatre a marble portrait head whose close-cropped hair and beard spoke of the third century after Christ; but when we washed the loam and incrusted lime from it, we noticed a different, earlier style of carving on the throat, lips, and ears, and on a little patch of hair at the top of the head, where it would not be seen from below. Apparently some theatrical angel, who, perhaps, had picked up the check for a redecoration of the theatre and wished to leave a tangible reminder of his benefaction, had engaged a sculptor to cut an old statue down into his own likeness. We can even recognize the man whose portrait it had originally been: the emperor Tiberius.

Columns have lent themselves to all manner of re-use. Greek masons usually built their columns in sections called drums. These were fastened together with metal pins soldered in place, and then carved with fluting. It was practically impossible to take down such a column without damaging the

Built in Augustus's day, this temple-in-the-round has been a Christian church since the Middle Ages. When Piranesi etched this view in 1758, it

was called Santo Stephano delle Carrozze because of the nearby wagon shops; it next became Santa Maria del Sole. Recently it has been restored

drums beyond repair, and consequently Greek columns were rarely re-used as such; when fire or earthquake or the crowbars of vandals had toppled them to the ground, scrap-metal dealers hurried to recover the metal. Badly smashed drums went into the limekiln, or into rubble masonry such as made up the medieval fortifications of the Acropolis.

In the north wall of the Acropolis are a score of marble drums that come from the unfinished Older Parthenon; you can still see the scorch-marks that were left on them when the Persians fired the scaffolding in 480 B.C. Also on the Acropolis is an Ionic drum that has been hollowed through for use as a wellhead; in the Roman Forum, near the temple of Romulus, is another almost identical with it. In Sant' Apollinare in Classe, at Ravenna, an ancient capital has been made over into a holy-water font.

Unlike Greek columns, Roman columns were regularly monolithic, with separate capitals and bases. Some of these were so firm and solid that they withstood the fires and other

The temple of Fortuna Virilis, recently restored, is a handsome example of Roman republican architecture. Piranesi depicted the structure when it served as a Christian church.

catastrophes which brought their superstructures crashing about them; and around the Forum you can still see a few such stalwart survivors soaring proudly into the sky.

Columns that fell were usually damaged beyond repair; it is inconceivable that the delicate leaves of Corinthian capitals, or the sharp edges of Ionic volutes, could survive a fall from any height. Yet the traveler who goes, guidebook in hand, through the churches of Italy will often find in those of the basilica type two rows of ancient columns supporting the roof. Other ancient columns turn up in porches, choirs, crypts, and bell towers. One can see them at Capua, Naples, Salerno, Amalfi, Otranto, Benevento, Ravenna, Trieste, Bologna, Lucca, Pisa—and in many other towns besides. Where the church plans called for more columns than were available in identical style and dimensions, the builders did not hesitate to put granite beside marble or to employ random sizes, raising too short columns on special bases (as for example in the Roman churches of Santa Maria in Aracœli and Santa Maria

in Trastevere, and in the porch of the cathedral at Terracina). This lighthearted approach to the problems of architecture gives a quaint charm to many Italian churches not otherwise distinguished.

In Rome alone, methodical listing, measurement, photographing, and analysis of all these re-used ancient columns, and an attempt to connect them with the Roman buildings from which they were taken, is a research problem of colossal dimensions still awaiting sponsorship. When the roof of an ancient structure fell, it usually brought down both the supporting walls and columns. Since fallen columns and capitals must be presumed to have been so badly damaged as to preclude re-use, the Roman buildings to which these intact columns originally belonged must have been still standing in the Middle Ages or later, when materials for the churches were being assembled; the builders, we therefore conclude, must have torn down scores of ancient Roman temples, basilicas, and porticoes.

This suggests that the familiar concept of medieval Rome as a vast field of ruins, after its successive devastations at the hands of Vandals, Goths, and Lombards, deserves reconsideration; despite the plundering, great numbers of imperial buildings must have continued to stand long after the political collapse of pagan Rome.

Not all the vandalism is to be charged to the Vandals. If the process has stopped, it has stopped only recently. In Rome, in the Piazza Colonna, the *palazzo* which used to house the famous Fagiano restaurant has a portico of delicate Ionic columns brought there from Veii in 1838, as the inscription on the entablature records; the inscription fails to say, of course, that if the Veii colonnade had not been standing up to the moment when the columns were taken, there would have been no columns fit to take.

Our excavations at Minturnae revealed a pattern of economic re-use which is typical of the whole Mediterranean world. Among our earliest finds in the forum were twenty-nine altars, dating from the first century B.C., dedicated to Venus, Ceres, Hope, and Mercury and inscribed with the names of slaves and freedmen who dedicated them and with their masters' names as well. These had been incorporated in the foundations of a temple built in the following century, by which time the dedicators were dead and forgotten and the altars represented twenty-nine handy blocks of stone already squared and ready for use; so into the temple they went.

On the other side of this temple was what looked like a well, but when we went poking in its throat we discovered that the bottom was blocked with large stones. It was not a real well but a bidental, a kind of tomb containing samples of buildings which had been struck by lightning; its purpose was to appease Jupiter by commemorating his wrath. We found a terra-cotta statue of Winged Victory that had stood on the roof of a small temple, two Tuscan capitals from a large temple, and a column drum from a portico. Other fragments had been used to build the well's masonry foundations; when

RIGHT: *A detail from the portico of the church of San Lorenzo fuori le Mura in Rome reveals a Roman column and cornice with a medieval mosaic and frieze.*

BELOW: *The Villa Medici (now the French Academy) in Rome was built in 1580 by Annibale Lippi, an architect of evident genius, as well as thrift. He decorated the rear façade with assorted antiquities, some of which had originally come from famous Roman monuments. The reliefs on the second story are mostly clever patchworks—an arm from here, a head from there. The bust of Jove in the niche at top left is a Roman copy of a Hellenistic work; his duplicate on the opposite tower is a 16th-century copy.*

This sturdy Roman goddess and stead-fast Christian saint were identical twins to begin with, but one of them was converted. The Vatican's statue of Juno at left and the Saint Helena at the church of Santa Croce in Gerusalemme in Rome are copies of the same lost Greek original. It may have been Bernini himself who sometime in the 17th century gave the second Juno a new head, new hands, and a cross and christened her Saint Helena.

we holed through the latter, in order to free the capitals and the drum, we found that the rubble included architectural terra-cottas from two or three forum buildings.

Under the floor of the scene building of the theatre at Minturnae, in back of the stage, we found thirty or so Christian tombs of the fifth century. These were mostly made of roof tiles from nearby buildings, but a couple were of finer material—marble revetment slabs that had been pried from the finery of the stage. One of the twenty-four masonry vaults which supported the auditorium of the theatre had served briefly as a little Christian chapel; face down on its floor was a fine bronze inscription of the chapel's benefactor.

Nearby we found a temple of Julius Caesar, built shortly after his death. Along both flanks of the temple were long, narrow troughs of postclassical masonry, placed so as to catch rain water dripping from the eaves; but until a Gothic devastation in A.D. 560, Minturnae's water supply had come by aqueduct from the great spring at Spigno; consequently, we assumed that these troughs would not have been needed before 560 and were thus built after that. We also deduced from this a useful archaeological fact—that the temple remained standing until after 560—for there would have been no purpose in building troughs to catch the drip from the roof unless there was a roof from which rain could drip. We felt sure that we were correct because when we found the temple walls, they were lying where they fell—on top of the troughs.

The trough to the west of the temple ran the whole length of the eaves, but the one to the east ran only halfway because the rest of the space had been pre-empted for a small temple of Venus. In trying to determine the ancient ground level in back of this temple, we went deeper than necessary and stumbled on the rarest of finds, a cache of broken terra-cotta statues from a small Italic pediment. When this deposit appeared to extend under the trough, we deemed it more valuable than the trough and decided to demolish the latter.

After photographing and measuring it carefully we summoned our best laborer, Giuseppe Imperatore, with his talented pickaxe. Giuseppe raised his pick high in the air and brought it down neatly in a crack in one corner of the masonry. The corner split open and out rolled a fine marble portrait head, which lay staring at the unaccustomed sunlight. To this day I swear it blinked.

In the tenth century A.D. a prince of Capua named Pandolfo Capodiferro built at the mouth of the Garigliano River, a mile below Minturnae, a watchtower against the Saracens. The soil there is all silt; there is no stone to be quarried. But Pandolfo's men found an abundance of cut stone in the deserted city. They loaded barges with all manner of limestone and marble from the ruins—architraves, lintels, cornices, columns, inscriptions, capitals, curbstones, sills—and built of these a white tower which was virtually a museum of the architectural decoration of Minturnae. Then, in World War II, it served one last purpose: the Germans defending the Garigliano line razed the tower and used its stones for bunkers.

But Pandolfo did not exhaust the Minturnae quarry: in the cathedral at Gaeta, a few miles away, are four ancient columns, one of which is inscribed COLON[IA] MINTVRN[EN-SIVM]. The medieval town of Traetto, now renamed Minturno, standing picturesquely and prudently on a hill a couple of miles back from the sea, was largely built of cut tufa blocks from the city walls of Minturnae. In the theatre at Minturnae we found three limekilns, where medieval masons seeking mortar and plaster for the building of Traetto had burned limestone seats and marble revetments from the theatre and forum. Two kilns were empty; the third had been charged but never fired. It was filled to the brim with bits of molding, pavement, sculpture, revetment, and a miscellany of scraps—all too shattered for any nobler use.

Marble sarcophagi lend themselves to a fine variety of re-uses. They make good bathtubs, watering troughs for farm

animals, tanks for steeping, vats for tanning and dyeing, wash-basins, and baptismal fonts.

A more natural thing to do, of course, was to use sarcophagi secondhand for their intended purpose: simply sweep out the dust of the original occupant and bury someone else in his place. In the Baptistry of Florence a thirteenth-century bishop named John of Velletri reposes in a Roman sarcophagus. At St. Peter's at least six popes have borrowed their tombs from pagans or early Christians. In Santa Maria sopra Minerva in Rome (built, as its name indicates, upon the ruins of an ancient temple of Minerva), one Giovanni Arberino is buried in a particularly famous sarcophagus whose sculpture shows Hercules strangling the Nemean Lion.

Large family tombs, the kind with domed or vaulted roofs and multiple chambers, are real property. A small peasant family can live comfortably in one, or at least use it as a stable for the animals. Others have found grander ends. On the Appian Way, just outside Rome, stands the imposing cylindrical tomb of the Roman matron Caecilia Metella. During the Renaissance the tomb was made into a fortress of the Caetani family, and it still has the battlements with which they equipped it.

The mausoleum of Augustus in Rome became, in the twelfth century, a fortress of the Colonnas; from 1907 until 1936 it was a concert hall, the Augusteo, famous throughout the musical world for the exquisite perfection of its acoustics —certainly not one of the possibilities foreseen by its architect. Perhaps the most famous re-used tomb of all is Hadrian's, now the Castel Sant' Angelo, which became successively a fortress, a papal residence, and a military museum.

Some large tombs were turned into churches: the mausoleum Constantine built at Rome for his daughter Constantia became the church of Santa Costanza in A.D. 1256. The tomb of Saint Helena, Constantine's queen, is the church of SS. Pietro e Marcellino, but the Empress's sarcophagus has been moved to the Vatican Museum. At Ravenna the mausoleum of Gallia Placidia, which still contains three of its sarcophagi, is the church of SS. Nazario e Celso; while the tomb of Theodoric the Great became Santa Maria della Rotonda.

Some great structures survived because an entire community moved into them. This is what happened to the palace that Diocletian built in Dalmatia before his abdication in A.D. 303. In later centuries this vast complex of structures housed virtually the entire community of Spalato (Split). At Palmyra, in Syria, the same thing occurred: when archaeologists first reached this desert oasis, they found the entire Arab village of Tadmor firmly lodged in the vast sanctuary of Baal. The amphitheatres of Verona in north Italy and of Nîmes and Arles in Provence (see above) owe their relatively good preservation to the circumstance that medieval communities moved into them en masse, erecting masonry houses in concentric ellipses on the rising seats and blocking the open arcades of the exteriors.

More often, however, entire buildings were dismantled to obtain their materials. The Themistoclean Wall at Athens, built in an emergency, was made of any material that came to hand—grave monuments, inscriptions, sculptures, and tombstones. Often the greatest builders were the most ruthless destroyers. Constantine, intent upon the embellishment of his new capital of Constantinople, despoiled Hadrian's villa, the most lavish country seat ever constructed, and gathered marbles and works of art from all over the Empire. We saw earlier how he obtained relief sculptures for his arch.

The wonder is not that so much has been lost, but that anything has survived.

The basilica, one of the most common of Western church plans, was likewise the plan of the typical Roman law court. The fact that early Christians so readily chose to adapt to their uses a secular building has suggested to some students that the form of the classical temple was deliberately avoided by Christian church builders. They argue that the temple was not suited to Christian worship: the pagan ritual was regularly performed outdoors, at an open-air altar in front of the temple, around which worshipers might gather to do homage to a god and witness an animal sacrifice. The temple itself was reserved for the god's personal use on his visits to the community; it contained his image and his treasure, but no part of the public service of worship was conducted there, and the laity was not welcome. Down to the time of Augustus, Roman temples had no steps; they stood on a high platform like a box, called a podium; if a priest or sexton had any legitimate business inside, he got someone to boost him up or sent for a ladder. Christian ritual, on the contrary, required space for regular congregational worship throughout the year in all seasons and weathers (and therefore indoors), where the parish could assemble to sing and pray in unison, listen to a sermon, and take communion. For this, the argu-

FROM *Antiquities of Athens* BY STUART AND REVETT, 1787

The Turks twice put up a mosque inside the Parthenon; the second one is shown in this English print of 1787. Damage to the pediment occurred a century earlier in an explosion.

ment goes, the temple cella was too small; a larger chamber was needed. Besides, were not pagan temples so contaminated with centuries of pagan ritual that no purification could cleanse them? The law courts, without religious connotations and meeting precisely the requirements of a large, sheltered, indoor area, were the obvious solution.

This is a perfectly reasonable-sounding argument until one assembles the facts. Why should the early Christians, who made an episcopal throne out of a chariot, or a baptismal font out of a sarcophagus, or a church out of a tomb, reject a well-constructed temple? The fact is that a great many temples, both Greek and Roman, were at one time or another remodeled as churches, and a fair number are still used as churches.

In Greece, for instance, the Parthenon became a Byzantine church, then a Roman Catholic church, then a Turkish mosque, and then a powder magazine. After the explosion that ensued, the Turks built a smaller mosque in the shell of

the building (left). The temple of Erechtheus, on the Acropolis, became first a church and later the harem of the Turkish governor. The temple of Hephaestus, overlooking the Agora, is, in its latter-day guise of Christian church, one of the three best preserved of all Greek temple buildings. We can see plainly how it was remodeled: because the entrance to a Greek temple was on the east while the entrance to a church is regularly on the west, it was necessary to block up the original east door of the temple and open a new one at the other end, cutting an opening through the rear cella wall and making a narthex or vestibule out of the opisthodome.

In Italy hundreds of Roman temples were taken over as churches. The Forum alone offers half a dozen examples. The Curia became the church of Sant' Adriano; part of the Library of Augustus became Santa Maria Antiqua; the temple of Antoninus and Faustina became San Lorenzo in Miranda (page 7); and in the sixth century A.D. the two adjoining temples of Sacra Urbs and the Divine Romulus were transformed into the church of SS. Cosma e Damiano.

We may say, then, that neither in Greece nor in Italy did the early Christians display any reluctance to convert ancient Greek and Roman temples, as well as basilicas, baths, tombs, and, later, mosques, into churches. Upon reflection, the argument that temple cellas were too small for congregational worship falls away. Some cellas were spacious enough for several hundred worshipers; some were small, but at the beginning of Christianity most congregations were small. The point is that anything capable of being re-used was normally put to new use, and this applies universally, to pagan temples as well as to scrap bronze.

But from this emerges another conclusion. It has been fashionable among Western critics to depict the early Christians as the great despoilers of ancient art, who in their haste to rid the scene of the emblems of pagan worship venomously ransacked and toppled temples, shrines, and statues. It may be true that some Christians, carried away by excess zeal, smashed heathen idols and did other damage which we should now regard as wanton; but as we have now seen, we are to attribute most destruction not to partisan spleen but to economic circumstance—poverty and the dire need to utilize every re-usable heritage.

Of the ancient Greek and Roman temples that have survived in good enough condition so that they can be seen and admired and studied in our own day, almost every one at some point in its history was taken over by Christians, who assumed the responsibility of keeping it clean, patching the masonry, repairing the roof from time to time, and locking the doors. Without this welcome paradox of history, we would have far less than we do of Greek and Roman temple architecture.

Well known as a lecturer and teacher, Jotham Johnson heads the Classics Department at New York University; he also presides over the Archaeological Institute of America.

LEFT: *The remote Turkish village of Geyre is built amid the ruins of Aphrodisias, an ancient Roman city which once sold statuary to all the Empire. The inhabitants of Geyre have picked up what they can: here a broken column is used to buttress a porch.*

BELOW: *The stones of antiquity have sometimes been re-used out of necessity, sometimes out of admiration. In Rome the architects who designed the magnificent new railway terminal (completed in 1950) found a particularly happy way to re-use, figuratively, a relic of the past. The line of the Termini's roof —and thus the concept of the building—was inspired by the shape of the Servian walls, to the left, which date from the 4th century B.C. and are named for Servius Tullius, one of the early kings of Rome.*

How does a scientist make his discoveries? How does a poet find his metaphors?

It is done, says this author, through THE

By ARTHUR KOESTLER

The act of creation, according to Arthur Koestler, is not defined in terms of its results, its products or works. It is defined, rather, as a certain way in which the mind functions, a particular manner whereby two seemingly unrelated patterns of behavior are brought together. Nor is this "bisociation," as Koestler calls it, the exclusive property of the "creative" artist: scientists and artists arrive at their discoveries in the same way—through the Eureka Process. In exploring the very nature of creativity—certainly no modest task—Koestler has produced at least one worthwhile by-product. He has constructed a bridge between what C. P. Snow has called the "two cultures" of the scientists and the humanists.

Born in Hungary in 1905, Koestler published one of his most distinguished novels, Darkness at Noon, *at the age of thirty-six, just after he had begun to write in English. He prides himself, as he once said, "on being the only writer who twice changed the language in which he writes: from Hungarian to German at the age of seventeen, from German to English at thirty-five." In his several languages Koestler has been a journalist, essayist, novelist, dramatist, and a theorist on art, science, and social ethics.*

The Act of Creation, *from which this article is taken, was published last spring in England. The book grows out of two earlier Koestler works,* The Sleepwalkers *and* Insight and Outlook. *It is to be published in America later this month by Macmillan. The book's appearance in Britain evoked spirited praise from English critics. In comparison with her colleagues, Jocelyn Brooke, writing in* Punch, *seemed almost sparing of her approval: "The number of subjects about which Mr. Koestler has at least a working knowledge, the innumerable authorities from whom he quotes, are astonishing in this age of increasing specialization. Nobody, today, can hope to 'take all knowledge for his province,' but there can be few aspects of the contemporary world which have entirely escaped Mr. Koestler."*

That animals can display originality and inventiveness has been asserted since Aesop, but was experimentally demonstrated for the first time by the German psychologist Wolfgang Köhler. In 1917 Köhler published *The Mentality of Apes,* an account of his experiments with chimpanzees on Tenerife which has since become a classic. Here is a characteristic description of an animal discovering the use of tools (my italics):

Nueva [a young female chimpanzee] was tested three days after her arrival (March 11. 1914). She had not yet made the acquaintance of the other animals but remained isolated in a cage. A little stick is introduced into her cage; she scrapes the ground with it, pushes the banana skins together in a heap. and then carelessly drops the stick at a distance of about three-quarters of a meter from the bars. Ten minutes later fruit is placed outside the cage beyond her reach. She grasps at it, vainly of course, and then begins the characteristic complaint of the chimpanzee: she thrusts both lips—especially the lower—forward for a couple of inches, gazes imploringly at the observer, utters whimpering sounds. and finally flings herself onto the ground on her back—a gesture most eloquent of despair. which may be observed on other occasions as well. Thus. between lamentations and entreaties, some time passes, until—about seven minutes after the fruit has been exhibited to her—she suddenly casts a look at the stick, ceases her moaning, seizes the stick, stretches it out of the cage, and succeeds, though somewhat clumsily, in drawing the bananas within arm's length. *Moreover, Nueva at once puts the end of her stick behind and beyond her objective. . . .* The test is repeated after an hour's interval; on this second occasion, the animal has recourse to the stick much sooner and uses it with more skill; and at a third repetition, the stick is used immediately.

It is obvious that Nueva was not led to her discovery by any process of conditioning, or trial and error. Her behavior from the moment when her eyes fell on the stick was, in Köhler's words, "unwaveringly purposeful"; she seized the stick, carried it without hesitation to the bars. stretched it out of the cage, and placed it behind the banana—a smooth, integrated sequence

16

EUREKA PROCESS

*"Had Sultan known Greek
he would certainly
have shouted 'Eureka!' "*

of actions, quite different from the erratic, hit-and-miss be-havior of rats trying to find their way through a maze, or cats trying to get out of a puzzle box. It was an original, self-taught accomplishment which had no precedent in the chimpanzee's past. The process that led to her discovery can be described as a synthesis of two previously unconnected skills, acquired in earlier life. In the first place, Nueva had learned to get at bananas outside her cage by squeezing an arm or foot through the bars; the ensemble of variations of this simple skill consti-tutes matrix number one.* She had also acquired the habit—matrix number two—of scraping the earth with a stick and of pushing objects about with it. But in this playful activity the stick was never used for any utilitarian purpose; to throw, push, or roll things about is a habit common to a variety of young animals. Nueva's discovery consisted in applying this playful habit as an auxiliary matrix to get at the banana. The moment

* Koestler uses the word "matrix" to denote "any ability, habit, or skill, any pattern of ordered behavior governed by a code of fixed rules."

of truth occurred when Nueva's glance fell on the stick while her attention was set on the banana. At that moment the two previously separate matrices fused into one, and the "stick to play with" became a "rake to reach with"—an implement for obtaining otherwise unobtainable objects.

Like many other discoveries, Nueva's seems a simple and obvious one—but only after the fact. A dog, for instance, will carry a stick between his teeth, but he will never learn to use it as a rake. However, chimpanzees are not the only species that find it possible to apply a "playful" technique to a utilitarian purpose with which it had not been connected in previous ex-perience; a number of discoveries in the history of human sci-ence consisted in just that. Galileo astonished the world when he turned the telescopic toys invented by Dutch opticians to astronomic use; the steam engine, which was invented as a mechanical toy by Hero of Alexandria in the second century A.D., had to wait fifteen hundred years before it was put to practical use; the geometry of conic sections, which Apollonius of Perga had studied in the third century B.C. just for the fun of it, gave Kepler, two thousand years later, his elliptical orbits of the planets; the passion for dice of the Chevalier de Méré made him approach Pascal for advice on a gambling system, and thus was the theory of probability born, that indispensable tool of modern physics and biology, not to mention the insurance busi-ness. "It is remarkable," wrote Pierre Simon de Laplace, "that a science which began with considerations of play has risen to the most important objects of human knowledge." Thus at the very start of our inquiry we hit on a pattern—the discovery that a playful or *l'art-pour-l'art* technique provides an unexpected clue to problems in a quite different field—which is one of the leitmotivs in the history of science.

Nueva's discovery was the use of tools; the next one to be described is the making of tools. Its hero is Sultan, the genius among Köhler's chimpanzees:

"He had melted his body down,
as it were . . . and he
could do the same with the crown."

(17 February 1914) Beyond some bars, out of arm's reach, lies an objective [a banana]; on this side, in the background of the experiment room, is placed a sawed-off castor-oil bush, whose branches can be easily broken off. It is impossible to squeeze the tree through the railings, on account of its awkward shape; besides, only one of the bigger apes could drag it as far as the bars. Sultan is let in, does not immediately see the objective, and, looking about him indifferently, sucks one of the branches of the tree. But, his attention having been drawn to the objective, he approaches the bars, glances outside, the next moment turns round, goes straight to the tree, seizes a thin slender branch, breaks it off with a sharp jerk, runs back to the bars, and attains the objective. From the turning round upon the tree up to the grasping of the fruit with the broken-off branch is one single quick chain of action, without the least hiatus and without the slightest movement that does not, objectively considered, fit into the solution described.

Had Sultan known Greek he would certainly have shouted "Eureka!" Köhler comments:

For adult man with his mechanized methods of solution, proof is sometimes needed, as here, that an action was a real achievement, not something self-evident; that the breaking off of a branch from a *whole tree,* for instance, is an achievement over and above the simple use of a stick is shown at once by animals less gifted than Sultan, even when they understand the use of sticks beforehand.

It has been said that discovery consists in seeing an analogy which nobody had seen before. Solomon discovered the analogy between the Shulammite's neck and a tower of ivory. Sultan discovered that a twisted branch on a tree with leaves on it had something in common with a straight, lifeless bamboo pole lying on the ground. What they had in common was very little: let us say that both looked "hardish" and "longish," but that is all. The branch, which previously was part and parcel of the tree, was wrenched out of its visual context—both figuratively and literally speaking—and made into a part of another, functional, context.

The now familiar shift of awareness to the previously unimportant "pole-like" aspect of the branch was very prettily demonstrated by another of Köhler's chimpanzees, Koko. It took Koko much longer to make the same discovery as Sultan; and when at last he had broken off a branch from the tree to use it as a stick, and marched with it toward the banana outside the cage, he

. . . eagerly picked off one leaf after the other, so that only the long, bare stem was left . . . The pulling off of the leaves is both correct and incorrect; *incorrect* because it does not make the stem any longer, *correct* because it makes its length show up better and the stem thus becomes optically more like a "stick." . . . There can be no doubt that Koko did not pull off the leaves in play only; his look and his movements prove distinctly that throughout the per-

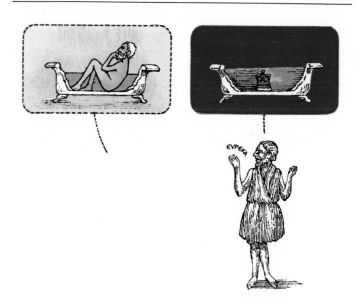

formance his attention is wholly concentrated on the objective [the banana]; he is merely concerned now with preparing the implement. Play looks quite different; and I have never seen a chimpanzee play while (like Koko in this case) he was showing himself distinctly intent upon his ultimate purpose.

Before either chimpanzee actually broke off the branch, there must have been a moment when he perceived it as a member *of both matrices at the same time*—still a part of the tree but already a detached tool. Thus one could say that Sultan and Koko had seen a *visual pun:* a single form (the branch) attached to two different functions.

The act of discovery has a disruptive as well as a constructive aspect. It must disrupt rigid patterns of mental organization to achieve the new synthesis. Sultan's habitual way of looking at the tree as a coherent visual whole had to be shattered. Once he had discovered that branches can be made into tools, he never again forgot it, and we may assume that a tree never again looked the same to him as before. He had lost the innocence of his vision, but from this loss he derived an immense gain: the perception of "branches" and the manipulation of "tools" were now combined into a single sensory-motor skill; and when two matrices have become integrated, they cannot be torn asunder. That is why the discoveries of yesterday are the commonplaces of today, and why we always marvel how stupid we were not to see what *post factum* appears to be so obvious.

Let me illustrate the last point by a human discovery which has much in common with Sultan's: the Principle of Archimedes. I must tell the story in a somewhat simplified form.

Hiero, tyrant of Syracuse and protector of Archimedes, had been given a beautiful crown, allegedly of pure gold, but he suspected that it was adulterated with silver. He asked Archimedes's opinion. Archimedes knew, of course, the specific weight of gold—that is to say, its weight per volume unit. If he could measure the volume of the crown, he would know immediately whether it was pure gold or not; but how on earth is one to determine the volume of a complicated ornament with all its filigree work? Ah, if only he could melt it down and measure the liquid gold by the pint, or hammer it into a brick of honest rectangular shape, or . . . and so on. At this stage he must have felt rather like Nueva, flinging herself on her back and uttering whimpering sounds because the banana was out of her grasp and the road to it blocked.

Blocked situations increase stress. Under its pressure the chimpanzee reverts to erratic and repetitive random attempts; in Archimedes's case we can imagine his thoughts moving round in circles within the frame of his geometrical knowledge and, finding all approaches to the target blocked, returning again and again to the starting point.

One day, while getting into his bath, Archimedes watched absent-mindedly the familiar sight of the water level rising from one smudge on the basin to the next as a result of the immersion of his body, and it occurred to him in a flash that the volume of water displaced was equal to the volume of the immersed parts of his own body—which therefore could simply be measured. He had melted his body down, as it were, without harming it, and he could do the same with the crown.

Once more, as in the case of the chimpanzee, the matter is childishly simple after the fact—but let us try to put ourselves in Archimedes's place. He was in the habit of taking a daily bath, but the experiences and ideas associated with it moved along habit-beaten tracks: the sensations of hot and cold, of fatigue and relaxation, and of a pretty slave girl massaging his limbs. Neither to Archimedes nor to anybody else before him had it ever occurred to connect the sensuous and trivial occupation of taking a hot bath with the scholarly pursuit of the measurement of solids. No doubt he had observed many times that the level of the water rose whenever he got into it; but this fact, and the distance between the two levels, was totally irrelevant to him—until it suddenly became bisociated* with his problem. At that instant he realized that the amount of rise of the water level was a simple measure of the volume of his own complicated body.

The solution may have been stimulated by a *verbal* concept (for instance: "rise of water level *equals* melting down of my solid body"); it may equally well have been a *visual* impression in which the water level was suddenly seen to correspond to the volume of the immersed parts of the body and hence to that of the crown—whose image was constantly lurking on the fringe of

* "Bisociation": Koestler's coinage for the rare "moment of truth" when two previously unconnected frames of reference (i.e., rise of water level in the bath and measurement of volume of solids) connect to create a new idea, as distinguished from routine associative thinking.

Archimedes's consciousness. The essential point is that at the critical moment *both* matrices were simultaneously active in his mind—though presumably on different levels of awareness. The creative stress resulting from the blocked situation had kept the problem on the agenda even while the beam of consciousness was drifting along quite another plane. Without this constant pressure, the favorable chance-constellation would have passed unnoticed—and joined the legion of man's missed opportunities for a creative departure from the stale habits of thought which numb his mental powers.

The sequel to the discovery is well known. Because of its picturesque appeal I shall occasionally refer to discovery in its psychological aspect as the "Eureka process" or "Eureka act."

Let us look at Archimedes's discovery from a different angle. When one climbs into a bath one *knows* that the water level will rise owing to its displacement by the body, and that there must be as much water displaced as there is body immersed; moreover, one mechanically estimates the amount of water to be let into the bath because of this expectation. Archimedes, too, must have known all this, but he had probably never before verbalized—that is, consciously formulated—this bit of knowledge. Yet *implicitly* it was there as part of his mental equipment; it was, so to speak, included in the code of rules of bath-taking behavior. Now we have seen that the rules which govern the matrix of a skill function on a lower level of awareness than the actual performance itself—whether it is playing the piano, carrying on a conversation, or taking a bath. We have also seen that the bisociative shock often has the effect of making such implicit rules explicit, of suddenly focusing awareness on aspects of experience which had been unverbalized, unconsciously implied, taken for granted; so that a familiar and unnoticed aspect of a phenomenon—like the rise of the water level—is suddenly perceived at an unfamiliar and significant angle. Discovery often means simply the uncovering of something which has always been there but was hidden from the eye by the blinkers of habit.

This applies equally to the discoveries of the artist who makes us see familiar objects and events in a strange, new, revealing light—as if piercing the cataract which dims our vision. Newton's apple and Cézanne's apple are discoveries more closely related than they seem.

Nearly all of Köhler's chimpanzees sooner or later learned the use of implements, and also certain methods of making implements. But a dog, however skillful in carrying a stick or a basket around, will never learn to use the stick to get a piece of meat placed outside its reach. We might say that the chimpanzees were *ripe* to discover the use of tools when a favorable chance-opportunity presented itself—such as a stick lying around just when needed. The factors which (among others) constitute ripeness for this type of discovery are the primates' manual dexterity and advanced oculomotor co-ordination, which enable them to develop the playful habit of pushing objects about with branches and sticks. Each of the separate skills, whose synthesis constitutes the new discovery, was well established previously and frequently exercised. In a similar way Archimedes's mental skill in manipulating abstract concepts like volume and density, plus his acute powers of observation, even of trivia, made him "ripe" for his discovery. In more general terms: the statistical probability of making a relevant discovery is the greater the more firmly established and well-exercised each of the still separate skills, or thought-matrices, are. This explains a puzzling but recurrent phenomenon in the history of science: that the same discovery is made, more or less at the same time, by two or more people; and it may also help to explain the independent development of the same techniques and similar styles of art in different cultures.

Ripeness in this sense is, of course, merely a necessary, not a sufficient, condition of discovery. But it is not quite such an obvious concept as it might seem. The embittered controversies between different schools in experimental psychology about the nature of learning and understanding can be shown to derive to a large extent from a refusal to take the factor of ripeness seriously. The propounders of behaviorist psychology were wont to set their animals tasks for which they were biologically ill-fitted, and thus to prove that new skills could be acquired only through conditioning, chaining of reflexes, learning by rote. Köhler and the Gestalt school, on the other hand, set their chimpanzees tasks for which they were ripe or *almost ripe,* to prove that all learning was based on insight. The contradictory conclusions at which they arrived need surprise us no more than the contrast between the learning achievements of a child of six months and a child of six years. This is a necessarily oversimplified description; the only point I wish to make is that the more ripe a situation is for the discovery of a new synthesis, the less need there is for the helping hand of chance.

Archimedes's eyes falling on the smudge in the bath or the chimpanzee's eyes falling upon the tree are chance occurrences of such high probability that sooner or later they were bound to occur; chance plays here merely the part of triggering off the fusion between two matrices by hitting on one among many possible appropriate links. We may distinguish between the *biological ripeness* of a species to form a new adaptive habit or acquire a new skill, and the ripeness of a *culture* to make and to exploit a new discovery. Hero's steam engine could obviously be exploited for industrial purposes only at a stage when the tech-

nological and social conditions made it both possible and desirable. Lastly (or firstly), there is the personal factor—the role of the creative individual in achieving a synthesis for which the time is more or less ripe.

The emphasis is on the "more or less." If ripeness were all—as Shakespeare and the Marxists affirm—the role of genius in history would be reduced from hero to midwife, who assists the inevitable birth; and the act of creation would be merely a consummation of the preordained. But the old controversy whether individuals make or are made by history acquires a new twist in the more limited field of the history of science. The twist is provided by the phenomenon of multiple discoveries. Historical research into this curious subject is of fairly recent origin; it came as a surprise when, in 1922, William F. Ogburn and Dorothy S. Thomas published some hundred and fifty examples of discoveries and inventions which were made independently by several persons; and, more recently, Robert K. Merton came to the seemingly paradoxical conclusion that "the pattern of independent multiple discoveries in science is . . . the dominant pattern, rather than a subsidiary one. . . ." He quotes as an example Lord Kelvin, whose published papers contain "at least thirty-two discoveries of his own which he subsequently found had also been made by others." The "others" include some men of genius such as Cavendish and Helmholtz, but also some lesser lights.

The endless priority disputes which have poisoned the supposedly serene atmosphere of scientific research throughout the ages, and the unseemly haste of many scientists to establish priority by rushing into print—or, at least, depositing manuscripts in sealed envelopes with some learned society—point in the same direction. Some—among them Galileo and Hooke—even went to the length of publishing half-completed discoveries in the form of anagrams, to ensure priority without letting rivals in on the idea. Köhler's chimpanzees were of a more generous disposition.

Thus one should not underestimate ripeness as a factor facilitating discoveries which, as the saying goes, are "in the air"—meaning that the various components which will go into the new synthesis are all lying around and only waiting for the trigger action of chance, or the catalyzing action of an exceptional brain, to be assembled and welded together. If one opportunity is missed, another will occur.

On the other hand, although the infinitesimal calculus was developed independently by Leibniz and by Newton, and a long line of precursors had paved the way for it, it still required a Newton or a Leibniz to accomplish the feat; and the greatness of this accomplishment is hardly diminished by the fact that two among millions, instead of one among millions, had the excep-

tional genius to do it. We are concerned with the question *how* they did it—the nature of creative originality—and not with the undeniable but trivial consideration that if they had not lived somebody else would have done it sometime; for that leaves the same question to be answered, to wit, *how* that someone else did it. I shall not presume to guess whether outstanding individuals such as Plato and Aristotle, Jesus of Nazareth and Paul of Tarsus, Aquinas, Bacon, Marx, Freud, and Einstein were expendable in the above sense, so that the history of ideas in their absence would have taken much the same course—or whether it is the creative genius who determines the course of history. I merely wish to point out that some of the major breakthroughs in the history of science represent such dramatic tours de force that "ripeness" seems a very lame explanation, and "chance" no explanation at all. Einstein discovered the principle of relativity "unaided by any observation that had not been available for at least fifty years before"; the plum was overripe, yet for half a century nobody came to pluck it. A less obvious example is Evariste Galois, one of the most original mathematicians of all times, who was killed in an absurd duel in 1832, at the age of twenty. On the night before the duel he revised a paper to the *Académie des Sciences* (which had previously rejected it as unintelligible); then, in a letter to a friend, he hurriedly put down a number of other mathematical discoveries. Jacques Hadamard, an eminent mathematician who has studied the psychology of invention in his field, reflects: "It was only after fifteen years that, with admiration, scientists became aware of the memoir which the Academy had rejected. It signifies a total transformation of higher algebra, projecting a full light on what had been only glimpsed thus far by the greatest mathematicians . . ." Furthermore, in the letter to his friend, Galois postulated a theorem which could not have been understood by his contemporaries because it was based on mathematical principles which were discovered only a quarter-century after his death. "It must be admitted . . ." Hadamard continues, "(1) that Galois must have conceived these principles in some way; (2) that they must have been unconscious in his mind, since he makes no allusion to them, though they by themselves represent a significant discovery."

This leads us to the problem of the part played by unconscious processes in the Eureka act.

Pythagoras, according to tradition, is supposed to have discovered that musical pitch depends on the ratio between the length of vibrating chords—the starting point of mathematical physics—by passing in front of the local blacksmith on his native island of Samos, and noticing that rods of iron of different lengths gave different sounds under the blacksmith's hammer. Instead of ascribing it to chance, we suspect that it was some obscure intuition which made Pythagoras stop at the blacksmith's shop. But how does that kind of intuition work? Here is the core of the problem of discovery—both in science and in art. I shall briefly describe, for the sake of contrast, two celebrated discoveries of entirely different kinds: the first apparently due to conscious, logical reasoning aided by chance; the second a classic case of the intervention of the unconscious.

Eighteen hundred and seventy-nine was the birth year of immunology—the prevention of infectious diseases by inoculation. By that time Louis Pasteur had already shown that cattle fever, rabies, silkworm disease, and various other afflictions were caused by microorganisms, and had firmly established the germ theory of disease. In the spring of 1879—he was fifty-six at that time—Pasteur was studying chicken cholera. He had prepared cultures of the bacillus, but for some reason this work was interrupted, and the cultures remained during the whole summer unattended in the laboratory. In the early autumn, however, he resumed his experiments. He injected a number of chickens with the bacillus, but unexpectedly they became only slightly ill and recovered. He concluded that the old cultures had been spoiled and obtained a new culture of virulent bacilli from chickens afflicted by a current outbreak of cholera. He also bought a new batch of chickens from the market and injected both lots, the old and the new, with the fresh culture. The newly bought chickens all died in due time, but, to his great surprise, the old chickens, who had been injected once already with the ineffective culture, almost all survived. An eyewitness in the lab described the scene which took place when Pasteur learned of this curious development. He "remained silent for a minute, then

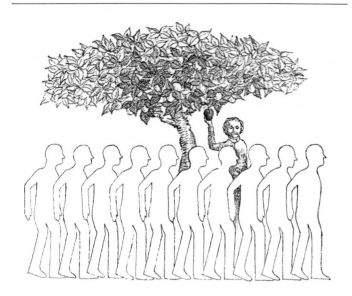

exclaimed as if he had seen a vision: 'Don't you see that these animals have been *vaccinated*!' "

Now I must explain that the word "vaccination" was at that time already a century old. It is derived from *vacca*, cow. Sometime in the 1760's a young medical student, Edward Jenner, was consulted by a Gloucestershire dairymaid who felt out of sorts. Jenner thought she might be suffering from smallpox, but she promptly replied: "I cannot take the smallpox because I have had the cowpox." After nearly thirty years of struggle against the skepticism and indifference of the medical profession, Jenner succeeded in proving the popular belief that people who had once caught the cowpox were immune against smallpox. Thus originated "vaccination"—the preventive inoculation of human beings against the dreaded and murderous disease with material taken from the skin sores of afflicted cattle. Although Jenner realized that cowpox and smallpox were essentially the same disease, which became somehow modified by the organism which carried it, he did not draw any general conclusions from his discovery. "Vaccination" soon spread to America and became a more or less general practice in a number of other countries, yet it remained limited to smallpox, and the word itself retained its exclusively bovine connotations.

The vision which Pasteur had seen at that historic moment was, once again, the discovery of a hidden analogy: the surviving chicks of the first batch were protected against cholera by their inoculation with the "spoiled" culture as humans are protected against smallpox by inoculation with pox bacilli in a modified bovine form.

Now Pasteur was well acquainted with Jenner's work. To quote one of his biographers, Dr. René Dubos (himself an

eminent bacteriologist): "Soon after the beginning of his work on infectious diseases, he became convinced that something similar to 'vaccination' was the best approach to their control. It was this conviction that made him perceive immediately the meaning of the accidental experiment with chickens."

In other words, he was "ripe" for his discovery, and thus able to pounce on the first favorable chance that offered itself. As he himself said: "Fortune favors the prepared mind." Put in this way, there seems to be nothing very awe-inspiring in Pasteur's discovery. Yet for about three-quarters of a century "vaccination" had been a common practice in Europe and America; why, then, did nobody before Pasteur hit on the "obvious" idea of extending vaccination from smallpox to other diseases? Why did nobody before him put two and two together? Because, to answer the question literally, the first "two" and the second "two" appertained to *different frames of reference*. The first was the technique of vaccination; the second was the hitherto quite separate and independent research into the world of micro-organisms: fowl parasites, silkworm bacilli, yeasts fermenting in wine barrels, invisible viruses in the spittle of rabid dogs. Pasteur succeeded in combining these two separate frames because he had an exceptional grasp of the rules of both, and was thus prepared when chance provided an appropriate link.

He knew—what Jenner knew not—that the active agent in Jenner's "vaccine" was the microbe of the same disease against which the subject was to be protected, but a microbe which in its bovine host had undergone some kind of "attenuation." And he further realized that the cholera bacilli left to themselves in the test tubes during the whole summer had undergone the same kind of "attenuation" or weakening as the pox bacilli in the cow's body. This led to the surprising, almost poetic, conclusion that life inside an abandoned glass tube can have the same debilitating effect on a bug as life inside a cow. From here on the implications of the Gloucestershire dairymaid's statement became gloriously obvious. Dubos has summarized, "As attenuation of the bacillus had occurred spontaneously in some of his cultures [just as it occurred inside the cow], Pasteur became convinced that it should be possible to produce vaccines at will in the laboratory. Instead of depending upon the chance finding of naturally occurring immunizing agents, as cowpox was for smallpox, vaccination could then become a general technique applicable to all infectious diseases."

One of the scourges of humanity had been eliminated—to be replaced in due time by another. For the story has a sequel with an ironic symbolism, which, though it does not strictly belong to the subject, I cannot resist telling. The most famous and dramatic application of Pasteur's discovery was his anti-rabies vac-

*"The vision which Pasteur had seen
at that historic moment was, once again,
the discovery of a hidden analogy . . ."*

cine. It was tried for the first time on a young Alsatian boy by name of Joseph Meister who had been savagely bitten on his hands, legs, and thighs by a rabid dog. Since the incubation period of rabies is ordinarily a month or more, Pasteur hoped to be able to immunize the boy against the deadly virus which was already in his body. After a dozen injections with rabies vaccine of increasing strength, the boy returned to his native village without having suffered any ill effects from the bites. The end of the story is told by Dubos: "Joseph Meister . . . later became gatekeeper of the Pasteur Institute [in Paris]. In 1940, fifty-five years after the accident that gave him a lasting place in medical history, he committed suicide rather than open Pasteur's burial crypt for the German invaders." He was evidently predestined to become a victim of one form of rabidness or another.

Now for a discovery of a diametrically opposite kind, where intuition plays the dominant part. The extracts which follow are from a celebrated lecture by Henri Poincaré at the *Société de Psychologie* in Paris, and concern one of his best-known mathematical discoveries: the theory of the so-called "Fuchsian functions." To reassure the reader I hasten to quote from Poincaré's own introductory remarks:

I beg your pardon; I am about to use some technical expressions, but they need not frighten you for you are not obliged to understand them. I shall say, for example, that I have found the demonstration of such a theorem under such circumstances. This theorem will have a barbarous name unfamiliar to many, but that is unimportant; what is of interest for the psychologist is not the theorem but the circumstances. . . .

And now follows one of the most lucid introspective accounts of the Eureka act by a great scientist:

For fifteen days I strove to prove that there could not be any functions like those I have since called Fuchsian functions. I was then very ignorant; every day I seated myself at my work table, stayed an hour or two, tried a great number of combinations, and reached no results. One evening, contrary to my custom, I drank black coffee and could not sleep. Ideas rose in crowds; I felt them collide until pairs interlocked, so to speak, making a stable combination. By the next morning I had established the existence of a class of Fuchsian functions, those which come from the hypergeometric series; I had only to write out the results, which took but a few hours.

Then I wanted to represent these functions by the quotient of two series; this idea was perfectly conscious and deliberate, the analogy with elliptic functions guided me. I asked myself what properties these series must have if they existed, and I succeeded without difficulty in forming the series I have called theta-Fuchsian.

Just at this time I left Caen, where I was then living, to go on a geologic excursion under the auspices of the School of Mines. The changes of travel made me forget my mathematical work. Having reached Coutances, we entered an omnibus to go some place or other. At the moment when I put my foot on the step the idea came to me, without anything in my former thoughts seeming to have paved the way for it, that the transformations I had used to define the Fuchsian functions were identical with those of non-Euclidean geometry. I did not verify the idea; I should not have had time, as, upon taking my seat in the omnibus, I went on with a conversation already commenced, but I felt a perfect certainty. On my return to Caen, for conscience' sake I verified the result at my leisure.

Then I turned my attention to the study of some arithmetical questions apparently without much success and without a suspicion of any connection with my preceding researches. Disgusted with my failure, I went to spend a few days at the seaside, and thought of something else. One morning, walking on the bluff, the idea came to me, with just the same characteristics of brevity, suddenness, and immediate certainty, that the arithmetic transformations of indeterminate ternary quadratic forms were identical with those of non-Euclidean geometry.

Returned to Caen, I meditated on this result and deduced the consequences. The example of quadratic forms showed me that there were Fuchsian groups other than those corresponding to the hypergeometric series; I saw that I could apply to them the theory of theta-Fuchsian series and that consequently there existed Fuchsian functions other than those from the hypergeometric series, the ones I then knew. Naturally I set myself to form all these functions. I made a systematic attack upon them and carried all the outworks, one after another. There was one, however, that still held out, whose fall would involve that of the whole place. But all my efforts only served at first the better to show me the difficulty, which indeed was something. All this work was perfectly conscious.

Thereupon I left for Mont Valérien, where I was to go through my military service; so I was very differently occupied. One day, going along the street, the solution of the difficulty which had stopped me suddenly appeared to me. I did not try to go deep into it immediately, and only after my service did I again take up the question. I had all the elements and had only to arrange them and put them together. So I wrote out my final memoir at a single stroke and without difficulty.

I shall limit myself to this single example; it is useless to multiply them. In regard to my other researches I would have to say analogous things . . .

Most striking at first is this appearance of sudden illumination, a manifest sign of long, unconscious prior work. The role of this unconscious work in mathematical invention appears to me incontestable. . . .

Similar experiences have been reported by other mathematicians. They seem to be the rule rather than the exception. One of these mathematicians is Jacques Hadamard:

. . . One phenomenon is certain and I can vouch for its absolute certainty: the sudden and immediate appearance of a solution at the very moment of sudden awakening. On being very abruptly awakened by an external noise, a solution long searched for appeared to me at once without the slightest instant of reflection on my part—the fact was remarkable enough to have struck me unforgettably—and in a quite different direction from any of those which I had previously tried to follow.

A few more examples. André Marie Ampère (1775–1836), after whom the unit of electric current is named, a genius of childlike simplicity, recorded in his diary the circumstances of his first mathematical discovery:

On April 27, 1802 [he tells us] I gave a shout of joy . . . It was seven years ago I proposed to myself a problem which I had not been able to solve directly, but for which I had found by chance a solution, and knew that it was correct, without being able to prove it. The matter often returned to my mind and I had sought twenty times unsuccessfully for this solution. For some days I had carried the idea about with me continually. At last, *I do not know how,* I found it, together with a large number of curious and new considerations concerning the theory of probability. As I think there are very few mathematicians in France who could solve this problem in less time, I have no doubt that its publication in a pamphlet of twenty pages is a good method for obtaining a chair of mathematics in a college.

The memoir did in fact get him a professorship at the *Lycée* in Lyon. It was called *Considerations of the Mathematical Theory of Games of Chance,* and demonstrated, among other things, that habitual gamblers are, in the long run, bound to lose.

Another great mathematician, Karl Friedrich Gauss, described in a letter to a friend how he finally proved a theorem on which he had worked unsuccessfully for four years:

At last two days ago I succeeded, not by dint of painful effort but so to speak by the grace of God. As a sudden flash of light, the enigma was solved. . . . For my part I am unable to name the nature of the thread which connected what I previously knew with that which made my success possible.

On another occasion Gauss is reported to have said: "I have had my solutions for a long time, but I do not yet know how I am to arrive at them." Paraphrasing him, György Pólya—a contemporary mathematician—remarks: "When you have satisfied yourself that the theorem is true, you start proving it."

We have seen quite a few cats being let out of the bag—the mathematical mind, which is supposed to have such a dry, logical, rational texture. As a last example I shall quote the dramatic case of Friedrich August von Kekule, Professor of Chemistry in Ghent, who, one afternoon in 1865, fell asleep and dreamed what was probably the most important dream in history since Pharaoh's seven fat and seven lean cows:

I turned my chair to the fire and dozed. Again the atoms were gamboling before my eyes. This time the smaller groups kept modestly in the background. My mental eye, rendered more acute by repeated visions of this kind, could now distinguish larger structures, of manifold conformation: long rows, sometimes more closely fitted together, all twining and twisting in snakelike motion. But look! What was that? One of the snakes had seized hold of its own tail, and the form whirled mockingly before my eyes. As if by a flash of lightning I awoke . . . Let us learn to dream, gentlemen.

The serpent biting its own tail gave Kekule the clue to a discovery which has been called "the most brilliant piece of prediction to be found in the whole range of organic chemistry" and which, in fact, is one of the cornerstones of modern science. Put in a somewhat simplified manner, it consisted of the revolutionary proposal that the molecules of certain important organic compounds are not open structures but closed chains or "rings" —like the snake swallowing its tail.

When life presents us with a problem, it will be attacked in accordance with the code of rules which enabled us to deal with similar problems in the past. These rules of the game range from manipulating sticks to operating with ideas, verbal concepts, visual forms, mathematical entities. When the same task is encountered under relatively unchanging conditions in a monotonous environment, the responses will become stereotyped, flexible skills will degenerate into rigid patterns, and the person will more and more resemble an automaton, governed by fixed habits, whose actions and ideas move in narrow grooves. He may be compared to an engineer who must drive his train along fixed rails according to a fixed timetable.

Vice versa, a changing, variable environment will tend to create flexible behavior patterns with a high degree of adaptability to circumstances—the driver of a motorcar has a greater degree of freedom than the engineer. But novelty can be carried to a point—by life or in the laboratory—where the situation still resembles *in some respects* other situations encountered in the past, yet contains new features or complexities which make it impossible to solve the problem by the same rules of the game which were applied to those past situations. When this happens we say that the situation is *blocked*—though the subject may realize this fact only after a series of hopeless tries, or never at all. To squeeze the last drop out of the metaphor: the motorist is heading for a frontier to which all approaches are barred, and all his skill as a driver will not help him—short of turning his car into a helicopter, that is, playing a different kind of game.

A blocked situation increases the stress of the frustrated drive. What happens next is much the same in the chimpanzee's case as in that of Archimedes. When all hopeful attempts at solving the problem by traditional methods have been exhausted, thought runs around in circles in the blocked matrix like rats in a cage. Next, the matrix of organized, purposeful behavior itself seems to go to pieces, and random trials make their appearance, accompanied by tantrums and attacks of despair—or by the distracted absent-mindedness of the creative obsession. That absent-mindedness is, of course, in fact single-mindedness; for at this stage—the "period of incubation"—the whole personality, down to the unverbalized and unconscious layers, has become saturated with the problem, so that on some level of the mind it remains active, even while attention is occupied in a quite different field—such as looking at a tree in the chimpanzee's case, or watching the rise of the water level. This condition remains until either chance or intuition provides a link to a quite different matrix, which bears down vertically, so to speak, on the problem blocked in its old horizontal context, and the two previously separate matrices fuse. But for that fusion to take place a condition must be fulfilled which I called "ripeness."

Concerning the psychology of the creative act itself, I have mentioned the following interrelated aspects of it: the displacement of attention to something not previously noted, which was irrelevant in the old and is relevant in the new context; the discovery of hidden analogies as a result of the former; the bringing into consciousness of tacit axioms and habits of thought which were implied in the code and taken for granted; the uncovering of what has always been there.

This leads to the paradox that the more original a discovery the more obvious it seems afterward. The creative act is not an act of creation in the sense of the Old Testament. It does not create something out of nothing; it uncovers, selects, reshuffles, combines, synthesizes already existing facts, ideas, faculties, skills. The more familiar the parts, the more striking the new

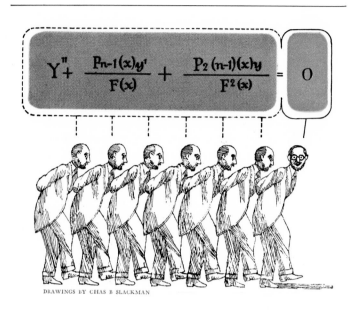

DRAWINGS BY CHAS B SLACKMAN

whole. Man's knowledge of the changes of the tides and the phases of the moon is as old as his observation that apples fall to earth in the ripeness of time. Yet the combination of these and other equally familiar data in Newton's theory of gravity changed mankind's outlook on the world.

"It is obvious," says Hadamard, "that invention or discovery, be it in mathematics or anywhere else, takes place by combining ideas. . . . The Latin verb *cogito* for 'to think' etymologically means 'to shake together.' St. Augustine had already noticed that and also observed that *intelligo* means 'to select among.' "

The "ripeness" of a culture for a new synthesis is reflected in the recurrent phenomenon of multiple discovery, and in the emergence of similar forms of art, handicrafts, and social institutions in diverse cultures. But when the situation is ripe for a given type of discovery, it still needs the intuitive power of an exceptional mind, and sometimes a favorable chance event, to bring it from potential into actual existence. On the other hand, some discoveries represent striking tours de force by individuals who seem to be so far ahead of their time that their contemporaries are unable to understand them.

Thus at one end of the scale we have discoveries which seem to be due to more or less conscious, logical reasoning, and at the other end those due to sudden insights which seem to emerge spontaneously from the depth of the unconscious. The same polarity of logic and intuition will be found to prevail in the methods and techniques of artistic creation. It is summed up by two opposite pronouncements: Thomas Edison's "one per cent inspiration and ninety-nine per cent perspiration," on the one hand, Picasso's *"je ne cherche pas, je trouve"* ("I do not seek—I find"), on the other.

Goodies, Girls, and Games

Pop Art, according to Lawrence Alloway, the critic who invented the term, is "the use of popular art sources by fine artists: movie stills, science fiction, advertisements, game boards, heroes of the mass media." To which might be added comic strips, circus posters, soup cans, beer cans, pinball machines, chocolate cream pies, animated cartoons, girls, girls, girls, and everything that Sears, Roebuck sells, including the kitchen sink. Does this mean Walt Disney is Pop Art? No, he's just Pop. The pictures in the Sears catalogue? *They* aren't art. The objects on these pages? A good question.

Pop Art is what swept the field during the 1963–64 art season, not only in New York but everywhere else—even in Sweden. Last March the Moderna Museet in Stockholm put on a big group show called "One Hundred and Six Forms of Love and Despair." The critics were cool ("American Pop Art is interesting as phenomenon and symptom, but mainly in a negative way"), but the public ate it up—a conditioned reflex, perhaps, to works like those opposite. However, a preoccupation with goodies is not the only characteristic of Pop Art. It is also banal (deliberately), garish, slapdash, funny (sometimes), satirical (occasionally), and vulgar (almost always).

In all this it accurately mirrors the machine-made, mass-produced environment—"slob culture," if you want to be harsh about it—in which almost everybody now lives. Pop Art's sheer recognizability may be one reason for its current popularity; it represents the most extreme reaction against the moody interior dramas of the abstract expressionists, whose noses are understandably out of joint. For Pop Art is nothing if not exterior. It takes the most blatant objects of the outside world and puts them down just as they are, with little attempt to transform them or even interpret them. The danger is that the public may not be able to tell the art from the artifact, as suggested in the following pages where various Pop works are set against Times Square shop windows and wallscapes that are virtually indistinguishable from them. We are, in short, pretty close to the moment when some enterprising gallery can exhibit wax ice-cream sundaes and get away with it, or—the living end?—bring in the real Miss Rheingold in all her sweetly standardized flesh and get a good price for her.

In the meantime, anything goes, everybody is having a high old time, the collectors are panting, the cash registers are jingling merrily. How long Pop will stay in art is a question. A contender with more serious views of American art may already be moving in from the exterior. It could be an offspring of Pop's.

Pop Art takes a "cool" view of our vulgar world

Wayne Thiebaud's Sandwich *(1963) is painted in creamy oils that are almost as thick and luscious as icing, while Claes Oldenburg's* Sundae *(1962) is made of enameled plaster plus a real glass, spoon, and plastic tray. In recent months both artists seem to have lost their sweet tooth: Thiebaud is painting people in the same glaring fluorescent light, and Oldenburg is making limp constructions of vinyl fabric that look like collapsed typewriters and telephones.*

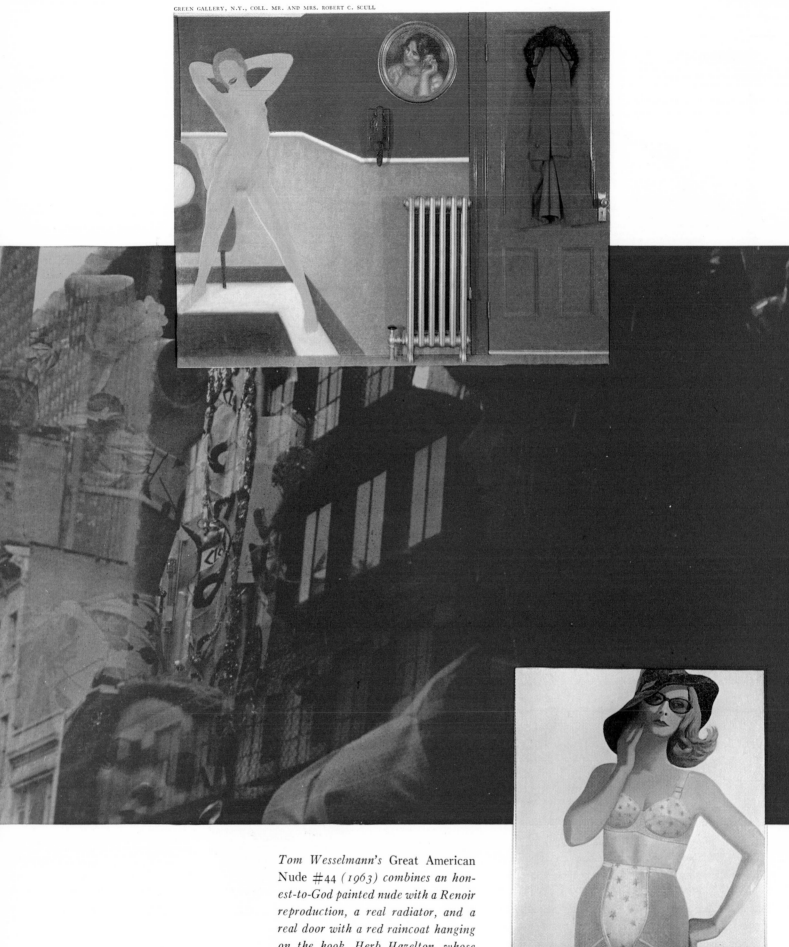

Tom Wesselmann's Great American Nude #44 *(1963) combines an honest-to-God painted nude with a Renoir reproduction, a real radiator, and a real door with a red raincoat hanging on the hook. Herb Hazelton, whose* Greta *(1963) is at the right, is a Los Angeles artist (born in Summit, N.J.) who has had a big success on the Coast with parodies of paintings like Manet's* Olympia *featuring Marilyn Monroe and Aunt Jemima, or Gainsborough's famous* Blue Boy *starring Elvis Presley.*

28

Roy Lichtenstein's paintings look exactly like blowups of comic strips—usually the soppy, soap-opera kind. By grossly magnifying these banal images, he calls attention to the emptiness and phoniness of popular culture. Most people get the point but ask the inevitable question, "Is it art?"—which he says is exactly what he wants them to do. Enough people think it is to make him one of the most successful of the Pop Artists, and undoubtedly the most controversial.

LEO CASTELLI GALLERY, N.Y.

Leo Jensen is a former rodeo cowboy who seems, happily, more interested in having fun with his gaudy wooden constructions than in delivering any kind of message. Baseball Machine *(below)* and The Lure of the Turf *(opposite)* are both gigantic, workable games. Jensen calls them *"functional toys,"* presumably because the purchaser can play with them whenever he gets tired of admiring them as sculptures—if that is the word—in the tradition of the cigar-store Indian.

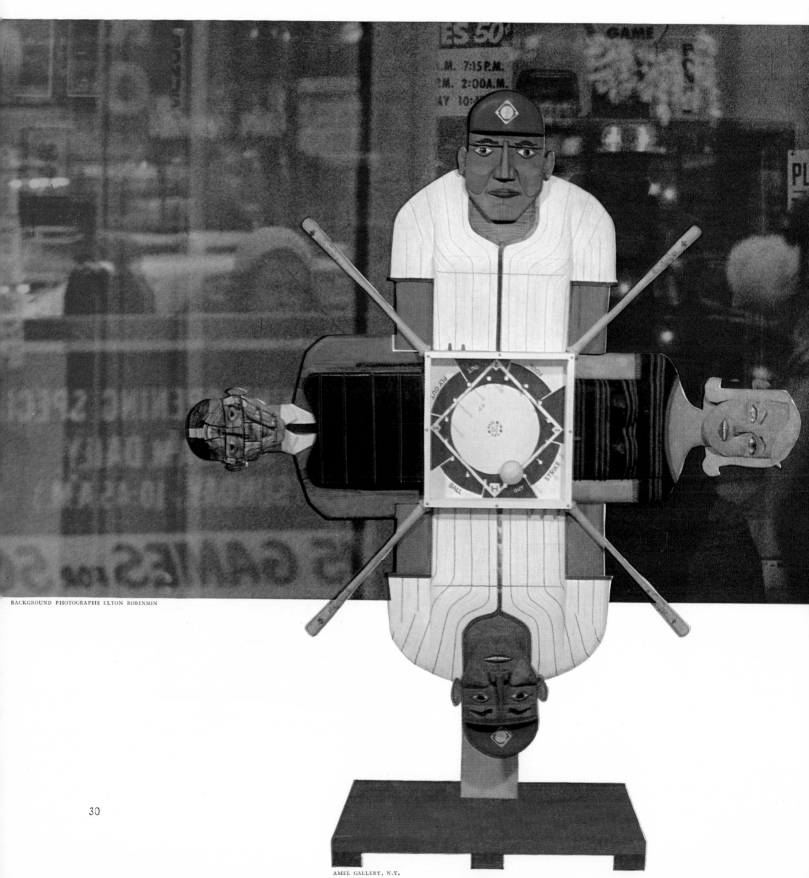

30

The Camper in the Back Yard

Although his cabin was only a mile and a half from home, and his sister brought him freshly baked cookies, Henry David Thoreau did find a wilderness by Walden and time to develop a sturdy, individualist's philosophy

It was in the early spring of 1845 that Henry David Thoreau went out to the shores of Walden Pond, a little glacial lake half a mile long and a third of a mile wide, two miles south of the village of Concord, Massachusetts, and began cutting down the tall, arrowy pines with which to build the cabin that was to make him famous around the world. He had long been thinking of such a move. As early as 1837 he had written in his *Journal*, "I seek a garret"; and in 1841, "I want to go soon and live away by the pond, where I shall hear only the wind whispering among the reeds." He wanted to get down to work on a book about the voyage he and his brother John had taken on the Concord and Merrimack rivers in 1839. And unless he could "get away from it all," it seemed as though that book would never be written.

There was plenty of precedent for Thoreau's taking to the woods. It was, after all, the period of the great migration west. Men, women, and children by the hundreds and thousands were pulling up stakes and moving to new territory to start life afresh. But Thoreau realized that he needed to change something more vital than his mere geographical location: he needed to change his way of life. He was going to stay in Concord and simplify his life there. Remembering what he had said so boastfully at his college graduation, he determined to reverse the Biblical instruction—to work one day a week and rest six, though rest would be only a euphemism. Those six days of each week he would devote to writing and the observation of nature.

Thoreau had already made several abortive attempts to simplify his life. In 1841 he had tried unsuccessfully to purchase the lonely Hollowell Farm on the outskirts of Concord. Shortly thereafter he had tried—again unsuccessfully—to obtain permission to build a cabin on Flint's Pond in nearby Lincoln. Then, in 1845, when he was twenty-seven, his opportunity came, and he did not let it go by. The preceding fall Ralph Waldo Emerson had purchased some land on the shores of Walden Pond. Ostensibly he bought it to save its trees from the woodcutter's axe, for it was a spot he loved and already one landowner there had permitted many trees to be felled along the shore of the pond. But Emerson had also long thought of building himself a rural study along these shores if the opportunity arose. And he thought, too, of giving the land to his sister-in-law, Lucy Jackson Brown, or to Bronson Alcott so they could build houses for their families. As it happened, neither house was ever started at the pond.

Then on March 5, 1845, Ellery Channing wrote Thoreau from New York City suggesting that he go out to Walden Pond, there build himself a hut, and begin the grand process of de-

By WALTER HARDING

Thoreau's cabin (above, in an engraving by W. H. W. Bicknell) was set twelve rods back from the shoreline (opposite) of Walden Pond

vouring himself alive. Thoreau quickly obtained permission from Emerson, went out to the pond late in March, and began to chop down the pines. Just how long he intended to live at the pond he had not decided, but it would be at least until he finished the book. "I went to the woods," he said, "because I wished to live deliberately, to front only the essential facts of life, and see if I could not learn what it had to teach, and not, when I came to die, discover that I had not lived. I did not wish to live what was not life, living is so dear; nor did I wish to practice resignation unless it was quite necessary. I wanted to live deep and suck out all the marrow of life, to live so sturdily and Spartan-like as to put to rout all that was not life, to cut a broad swath and shave close, to drive life into a corner, and reduce it to its lowest terms, and, if it proved to be mean, why then to get the whole and genuine meanness of it and publish its meanness to the world; or if it were sublime, to know it by experience, and be able to give a true account of it in my next excursion."

Thoreau began his work at the pond with a borrowed axe. It probably belonged to Bronson Alcott, although after its fame spread it was claimed by both Emerson and Channing. But from whomever he obtained it, he returned it later, he boasted, sharper than when he had borrowed it. He hewed the main timbers, he said, "six inches square, most of the studs on two sides only, and the rafters and floor timbers on one side, leaving the rest of the bark on, so that they were just as straight and much stronger than sawed ones." By mid-April he had every plank mortised and tenoned and the house framed, ready for raising. Meanwhile, for $4.25, he purchased an old shanty from James Collins, an Irish laborer on the Fitchburg Railroad. In a few hours he dismantled the shack, spread out the boards in the sun to bleach them and warp them back into shape, and drew the nails. Those nails, however, disappeared into the capacious pockets of one neighbor Seeley, who helped himself when Thoreau's back was turned.

It took Thoreau only two hours to dig a cellar hole six feet square and seven deep in the soft sandy soil, two hundred feet up a gentle slope from the shore of a cove on the north side of the pond, and in the shade of some small pines at the edge of a brier field. It was not a lonely spot. The well-traveled Concord-Lincoln road was within sight across the field; the Fitchburg Railroad steamed regularly along the opposite shore of the pond; Concord village was less than two miles away; and the house where Thoreau's parents lived was even closer along the railroad right of way.

In early May, adopting the old country custom, Thoreau invited some of his neighbors to help set up the frame of the house and raise the roof—both tasks that took more than one pair of hands. His assistants were a distinguished crew; they included Emerson, Bronson Alcott, Ellery Channing, George William Curtis (who later became editor of *Harper's Weekly*) and his brother Burrill, and Thoreau's favorite Concord farmer, Edmund Hosmer, and Hosmer's sons John, Edmund, and Andrew.

Thoreau was in no haste to move in. Once the frame was up, he did the remaining carpentry slowly, living in the meantime with his parents and walking back and forth to the pond each day, carrying his lunch wrapped in a paper. When warmer weather came, he cleared the brier field and planted two and a half acres, with beans and potatoes for money crops, and with corn, peas, and turnips for his own use.

On July 4, 1845—Independence Day, appropriately enough —he borrowed a hayrack to cart his few articles of furniture out to the cabin and moved in. As yet he had no chimney nor fireplace, and the walls, still unplastered, had wide chinks that let in the cool air at night. Later, when he had completed the cabin, he described it as "a tight shingled and plastered house, ten feet wide by fifteen long, and eight-feet posts, with a garret and a closet, a large window on each side, two trap doors, one door at the end, and a brick fireplace opposite." Out back was a woodshed. Close by— Thoreau was too much the Victorian to say exactly where—was a privy. The pond was his bathtub and refrigerator. And the spring under nearby Brister's Hill provided his drinking water when the pond was too warm.

The cabin cost Thoreau exactly $28.12½; his only extravagance was $3.90 for nails. Despite his boasted dexterity, he was apparently a bad shot with a hammer, and when the site of the Walden cabin was excavated a few years ago, the cellar hole was found filled with hundreds of bent nails.

Ellery Channing, who visited the cabin often, has aptly described it as a wooden inkstand on the shores of Walden Pond. "Just large enough for one . . . a durable garment, an overcoat, he had contrived and left by Walden, convenient for shelter, sleep, or meditation."

The inside of the cabin was as simple as the outside. Thoreau's total furniture, much of it homemade, consisted of a "bed, a table, a desk, three chairs, a looking glass three inches in diameter, a pair of tongs and andirons, a kettle, a skillet, and a frying pan, a dipper, a washbowl, two knives and forks, three plates, one cup, one spoon, a jug for oil, a jug for molasses, and a japanned lamp." For a time he kept three pieces of limestone on the desk, but threw them out when he found they required daily dusting. When a friend offered a mat for the floor, he declined it, saying he did not want to spare the room for it nor the time to shake it out.

In the fall of 1845 he built a fireplace and chimney in his cabin. Using a thousand secondhand bricks, and stones and sand from the pond shore in his mortar, he worked slowly at his task, laying a few rounds of bricks a day. It was November before the task was completed. Meanwhile he took in a boarder for two weeks—his friend Ellery Channing. They found the tiny cabin so crowded that Channing spent the nights sleeping on the floor underneath Thoreau's low-slung cot.

With the coming of cold weather, Thoreau set about making the cabin more snug. He lathed the interior and then, gathering clean white sand from the opposite shore of the pond, he plastered all the walls. The previous winter he had burned a few clamshells to prove to himself that he could manufacture his own lime, but having satisfied himself that he could, he now bought two casks of lime for $1.20 each. From November 12 until December 6, while he was applying the plaster and letting it dry, he lived at home with his parents. It is a wonder that, having left it to dry in a cold building, he did not find it frozen and disintegrated on his return.

Thoreau ate simply and plainly while he lived at the pond. One of the Hosmers, who spent a Sunday in September of 1845 with him, said his "hospitality and manner of entertainment were unique, and peculiar to the time and place. The cooking apparatus was primitive and consisted of a hole made in the earth and inlaid with stones, upon which the fire was made, after the manner at the seashore when they have a clambake." Their meal included roasted horned pout, corn, beans, bread, salt, and so on. Hosmer gave the menu in English, and Thoreau rendered it in French, Latin, and Greek. "The beans had been previously cooked. The meal for our bread was mixed with lake water only . . . spread upon the surface of a thin stone . . . and baked. . . . When the bread had been sufficiently baked, the stone was removed, then the fish placed over the hot stones and roasted—some in wet paper and some without—and when seasoned with salt, were delicious."

When the fireplace was completed, Thoreau moved his cooking indoors. In his second year at the pond he gave up the fireplace and installed a small stove. It was not as poetic as the fireplace, and he felt that he had lost a companion. But he did not own a forest to burn, he said, and the stove was much more efficient.

*A*t the end of his first eight months at the pond he found that he had spent a total of only $8.74 for food—an average of twenty-seven cents a week. Clothing for the same period cost him only $8.40¾ and lamp oil two dollars. From an economic standpoint the experiment at Walden was a success.

There were those who complained that he balanced his budget by sponging on his friends and relatives. Some Concordians claimed that "he would have starved, if it had not been that his sisters and mother cooked up pies and doughnuts and sent them to him in a basket." It is true that his mother and sisters made a special trip out to the pond every Saturday, carrying with them each time some delicacy of cookery which was gladly accepted. And it is true that he raided the family cookie jar on his frequent visits home. But any other behavior on his part would have hurt his mother's feelings: she prided herself on her culinary accomplishments and dearly loved to treat her son.

The Emersons, too, frequently invited him to dinner, as did the Alcotts and the Hosmers. They had all done so before he went to Walden Pond and continued the custom after he left. Rumor had it that every time Mrs. Emerson rang her dinner bell, Thoreau came bounding through the woods and over the fences to be first in line at the Emerson dinner table. The fact that a mile and a half was an exceptional distance to hear a dinner bell was ignored by the gossips. In *Walden* Thoreau wrote, "If I dined out occasionally, as I had always done, and I trust shall have opportunities to again, it was frequently to the detriment of my domestic arrangements."

Thoreau found plenty to do at the pond. He learned to love having a broad margin to his life. On summer mornings he would sometimes sit in his sunny doorway from sunrise until noon, rapt in reverie, while the birds sang around him or flitted noiselessly through his house. He grew on such occasions, he thought, like corn in the night, and said his hours of idleness were not time subtracted from his life, but so much over and above his usual allowance. Other mornings he devoted to housework, setting all the furniture out on the grass, dashing water on the floor and scrubbing it with a broom and white sand from the pond shore, and returning the furniture to its place before the villagers had had their breakfast.

But most mornings he devoted to his garden. His bean rows added up to more than seven miles in length and required constant weeding. What is worse, the woodchucks nibbled the bean sprouts faster than he could pull the weeds. "My enemies," he said, "are worms, cool days, and most of all woodchucks. They have nibbled for me a quarter of an acre clean. I plant in faith, and they reap."

Thoreau was at a loss for a time what to do about it—the woodchucks, he felt, had prior claims as residents, but if they remained, there would be no garden. He finally consulted a veteran trapper for advice. "Mr. W., is there any way to get woodchucks without trapping them with—" "Yes; shoot 'em, you damn fool," was the reply. But Thoreau ignored that sage advice, and matters got worse instead of better. Finally, in desperation, he procured a trap and captured the grandfather of all woodchucks. After detaining it for several hours, he delivered it a severe lecture and released it, hoping never to see it again. But it was a vain hope. Within a few days it was back at its old stand, nibbling at the beans as heartily as ever. He set the trap again, and this time when he caught the villain, he carried it a couple of miles away, gave it a severe admonition with a stick, and let it depart in peace. He never saw the woodchuck again, but what the farmers in *that* area thought is not recorded.

On a later occasion when another woodchuck trifled with his garden, Thoreau was more bloodthirsty. Abandoning his not-too-strongly-held vegetarian principles, he trapped it, killed it, and ate it as a culinary experiment, reporting the meat surprisingly good.

Despite the woodchucks, the worms, the cool weather, and the weeds, Thoreau's garden was a success. His expenses for tools, plowing, seeds, and cultivator totaled only $14.72½. The garden yielded twelve bushels of beans, eighteen bushels of potatoes, and some peas (the sweet corn and turnips failed to mature). Keeping enough for his own needs, he sold beans, potatoes, grass, and stalks for a total of $23.44. Thus he had his food for a year and a profit of $8.71½. Comparatively speaking, he thought, few Concord farmers did as well.

The second summer at Walden, Thoreau decided he had had

enough of agriculture, and so he planted only a third of an acre of garden—just enough for his own use. "I learned from my two years' experience," he explained, "that if one would live simply and eat only the crop which he raised, and raise no more than he ate, and not exchange it for an insufficient quantity of more luxurious and expensive things, he would need to cultivate only a few rods . . ."

In the colder seasons he found other methods of earning a living. For a dollar a day he did fence building, painting, gardening, and carpentering. Once he built a fireplace for a man who would not accept his protests that he was not a professional mason. On another occasion he built a woodshed "of no mean size" for six dollars and cleared half that sum by close calculation and swift work. Going home from one task he suffered a misfortune. As he was about to clamber into a hayrack, he inadvertently frightened the horse with his ubiquitous umbrella. Feet flew, the bucket on Thoreau's arm was smashed, and Thoreau himself was stretched out on his back on the ground. The sudden bending of his body backward strained his stomach muscles, and for a time he had to give up hard manual labor. He also tried his hand at surveying, making use of borrowed instruments and those left over from his schoolteaching days. He found the work both satisfying and remunerative; it enabled him simultaneously to earn a living and to spend most of his time out-of-doors in the fields and woods he loved. The only flaw was that his surveying was all too often a preliminary to woodcutting on the part of his employers, and thus he was playing his part in the destruction of the Concord woods. That fact was to disturb his conscience for some time.

From all these various sources Thoreau found he was easily able to support himself at the pond by working, at the most, six weeks a year. "In short," he wrote his friend Horace Greeley, "I am convinced, both by faith and experience, that to maintain one's self on this earth is not a hardship but a pastime, if we will live simply and wisely. . . . It is not necessary that a man should earn his living by the sweat of his brow, unless he sweats easier than I do."

A good part of his new-found free time he was able to devote to writing. The first work he completed at the pond was an extended essay on Thomas Carlyle. As early as 1842 he had begun making notes on Carlyle's works, but it was probably not until he got to the pond that he gathered the notes together and wrote the essay, which he tried out as a lecture before the Concord Lyceum on February 4, 1846. Although it was apparently a success, it was not what his townsmen expected or wanted to hear. They wanted to know why he, a college graduate, had given up conventional life and gone to live in a cabin in the woods. And so it was that Thoreau started writing the series of lectures that eventually grew into his masterpiece, *Walden, or Life in the Woods.* "Some," he said, "have asked what I got to eat; if I did not feel lonesome; if I was not afraid; and the like. Others have been curious to learn what portion of my income I devoted to charitable purposes; and some, who have large families, how many poor children I maintained." And those were among the questions he attempted to answer in his lectures and in his book.

It was a year later, February 10, 1847, before he delivered the first of these Walden lectures to his townsmen. That evening he read a paper entitled "A History of Myself"—a portion of which was eventually to become the "Economy" chapter of *Walden*—and it was received so well that, quite out of keeping with the regular practice of the Lyceum, he was asked to repeat it a week later for those who had missed it. Prudence Ward, who boarded at the Thoreau house, reported that "Henry repeated his lecture to a very full audience. . . . It was an uncommonly excellent lecture—tho' of course few would adopt his notions—I mean as they are shown forth in his life. Yet it was a very useful lecture, and much needed."

The favorable reactions to this and following lectures persuaded Thoreau that it would be worthwhile to write a book-length account of his life at the pond. So earnestly did he set to work that by September, 1847, he had completed the first draft. (It was seven years and eight complete revisions later, however, before the book was finally published.)

*M*eanwhile, Thoreau had not forgotten that one of his purposes in coming to Walden was to write another book, the account of his voyage on the Concord and Merrimack. Work on this, too, had progressed so rapidly that just a year from the time he moved to the pond the first draft was completed. Emerson immediately urged him to submit it to a publisher, but Thoreau insisted on taking further time to polish the manuscript. He spent a good many hours at the cabin reading various drafts aloud to such friends as Alcott and Emerson to get the benefit of their criticism. It was 1849 before the book was published. But the bulk of both it and *Walden* was written during his two years at the pond.

Thoreau still had time for strolling through the woods and fields of Concord or boating on its ponds and rivers. Evenings he often rowed out on the pond and played his flute or fished. He was, in his own words, "self-appointed inspector of snowstorms and rainstorms . . . surveyor, if not of highways, then of forest paths and all across-lot routes." He "looked after the wild stock of the town" and "had an eye to the unfrequented nooks and corners of the farm." In the fall he often went graping to the river meadows or hunting for nuts in the chestnut groves of Lincoln. In the first winter he dragged home old logs and stumps to burn in his fireplace.

He became fascinated with the phenomena of the pond. In the spring of 1846, before the ice broke up, he surveyed carefully the size and depth of the pond. He cut holes in the ice and charted his findings with a cod line and pound-and-a-half stone, a compass, and a chain. Native Concordians had sworn that the pond had no bottom, but he quickly put an end to their stories and proved that Walden had a reasonably tight bottom at a not unreasonable, though an unusual, depth. When, a century later, a trained limnologist checked the pond with the latest complex instruments, he was astounded to learn how accurate Thoreau's findings had been.

In February of 1847 Frederic Tudor, the "king" of the New England ice industry, took over the pond for a time. He and his former partner, Nathaniel Jarvis Wyeth, had quarreled. For years they had garnered huge profits by cutting ice near Boston and shipping it to warmer climates ranging from New Orleans to Calcutta. Now Wyeth gained control of the ice-cutting rights on most of the ponds they had been using. Rather than give in, Tudor moved farther from his base and purchased the rights to Walden Pond from Emerson and the Fitchburg Railroad. Shortly afterward a hundred Irish laborers and their Yankee supervisors began coming daily from Cambridge on the railroad. They often harvested as much as a thousand tons a day, stacking it up in a pile thirty-five feet high, banking it with hay, and covering it with boards. Thoreau was delighted. Here was one commercial venture that could do no harm to his pond or his woods, and the ice cutters, he thought, were a merry race, full of jest and sport. When he talked with them, they good-naturedly invited him to help saw the ice and, when the men fell into the water—which they did frequently—he invited them to use his cabin for a warming hut.

Inspired by their activities, he began a study of the temperature of Walden and the various nearby ponds, rivers, and springs. It was the first of the many statistical studies that were to become so much a part of his life. Like many of his contemporaries, he found himself developing a mania for charts of temperatures, heights, depths, weights, and dates. It disturbed him, but he was never able to free himself from the habit. (As for the ice, Tudor's men returned briefly in July and removed a small part of it, but Tudor had won his war and the pile was soon abandoned, not to melt away completely until September of the following year.)

The icemen were by no means Thoreau's only visitors. Hardly a day went by that he did not visit the village or was not visited at the pond. Shortly after Thoreau arrived, five of the workmen on the nearby Fitchburg Railroad dropped in to see what he was doing. When he told them of his plans, one replied: "Sir, I like your notions. I think I shall live so myself. Only I should like a wilder country, where there is more game. I have been among the Indians near Appalachicola. I have lived with them. I like your kind of life. Good day. I wish you success and happiness."

Before the second day was over, his sister Sophia arrived for a visit. She had so worried about him that she had not slept the previous night and now used the excuse of bringing out some food to reassure herself that he had survived what she thought of as the rigors of the wilds. But she soon got over her worries, and he made a point of stopping off regularly at his parents' house to reassure them all.

One of his most frequent visitors was Alek Therien, the French-Canadian wood chopper later immortalized in *Walden.* Therien, almost exactly Thoreau's age, had come down from Canada when he was in his teens. Although their backgrounds were very different,

Ralph Waldo Emerson's son, Dr. Edward Emerson, made this sketch of Thoreau from memory, apparently in 1917. Previously unpublished, it is reproduced here by permission of the Concord Free Public Library.

they found much in common. Thoreau admired Therien's overflowing happy nature and the thorough way he went about his work with his axe. Therien delighted in stealing up to Thoreau's cabin from the rear, firing off a stout charge in his gun, and laughing at Thoreau's surprise. Although Therien had had little formal education, he was keen and alert. The two often talked of books. Quite naturally their discussion turned to one of Thoreau's favorite authors—Homer. And when Therien told Thoreau that he thought Homer a great writer, "though what his writing was about he did not know," Thoreau took down his *Iliad* and translated portions for him. Therien was so delighted that he later quietly borrowed Pope's translation from the cabin and forgot to return it. Thoreau was to wonder in *Walden* where it had gone.

Emerson was, of course, a frequent visitor at the cabin, and showed his pleasure in Thoreau's experiment by making out a new will naming him heir to the land on which the cabin was built. When there was a threat of further woodcutting at the pond, Emerson purchased an additional forty-one acres on the Lincoln side of the pond and Thoreau was asked to witness the signing of the deed. Meanwhile Emerson frequently asked Thoreau to come in to the village to help him. When he found he was to be out of town for a few days, he asked Thoreau to supervise the building of a house for Mrs. Lucy Jackson Brown near his own. When he purchased two acres adjacent to his house, he asked Thoreau to survey it and gave him a dollar for his trouble. When he wanted the yard beautified, Thoreau dug up seventy-three pines, hemlocks, and junipers in the Walden woods and transplanted them to an area surrounding Emerson's house. It was then that Emerson said, "It is worthwhile to pay Henry surveyor's wages for doing other things. He is so thoughtful and he does so much more than is bargained for. When he does anything, I am sure the thing is done."

But not all was work between them. On pleasant summer days Thoreau would often join the Emerson family on a picnic or a blueberrying party. Emerson would drive a carryall with his mother and Mrs. Brown; Thoreau would follow in a hayrack loaded with the Emerson children and their friends, the mothers, and the Emerson servants. While Emerson and the ladies sat in the shade, Thoreau would lead the children from one berry bush to another.

Nathaniel Hawthorne, too, as long as he remained in Concord, frequently came out to the pond for a visit. With his almost painful shyness, he sometimes found Thoreau's cabin a welcome relief from the stream of visitors at home. Bronson Alcott was another frequent visitor. He purchased a farm on Lexington Road and set about restoring it. Thoreau helped him transplant evergreens and vines from the Walden woods and climbed a tree to assure him that the site he planned for a new summerhouse would have a good view. Thoreau often attended Alcott's "Conversations" in town. And Alcott, in his turn, spent nearly every Sunday evening for several months in the winter of 1846–47 visiting with Thoreau at his cabin.

Louisa May Alcott was a child at the time of Thoreau's residence at Walden, but he made an indelible impression on her and years later she recalled that he "used to come smiling up to his neighbors, to announce that the bluebirds had arrived, with as much interest in the fact as other men take in messages by the Atlantic cable. On certain days, he made long pilgrimages to find 'the sweet rhodora in the wood,' welcoming the lonely flower like a long-absent friend. He gravely informed us once, that frogs were much more confiding in the spring, than later in the season; for then, it only took an hour to get well acquainted with one of the speckled swimmers, who liked to be tickled with a blade of grass, and would feed from his hand in the most sociable manner."

The Alcotts often took their friends out to the pond to see Thoreau. Frederick L. H. Willis, who is said to be the original of Laurie in Louis May Alcott's *Little Women*, visited Thoreau in July of 1847, and recalled:

He gave us a gracious welcome, asking us within. For a time he talked with Mr. Alcott in a voice and with a manner in which, boy as I was, I detected a something akin with Emerson. He was a tall and rugged-looking man, straight as a pine tree. His nose was strong, dominating his face, and his

Thoreau's handwritten title page for Walden *was reproduced in 1909 in a limited edition of the book. Ticknor and Fields, the publishers of the original 1854 edition, had omitted the concluding quotation and moved Thoreau's prefatory note into the main body of the book.*

eyes as keen as an eagle's. He seemed to speak with them, to take in all about him in one vigorous glance. . . .

He was talking to Mr. Alcott of the wild flowers in Walden woods when, suddenly stopping, he said: "Keep very still and I will show you my family." Stepping quickly outside the cabin door, he gave a low curious whistle; immediately a woodchuck came running toward him from a nearby burrow. With varying note, yet still low and strange, a pair of gray squirrels were summoned and approached him fearlessly. With still another note several birds, including two crows, flew toward him, one of the crows nestling upon his shoulder. I remember it was the crow resting close to his head that made the most vivid impression upon me, knowing how fearful of man this bird is. He fed them all from his hand, taking food from his pocket, and petted them gently before our delighted gaze; and then dismissed them by different whistling, always strange and low and short, each little wild thing departing instantly at hearing its special signal.

Then he took us five children upon the Pond in his boat, ceasing his oars after a little distance from the shore and playing the flute he had brought with him, its music echoing over the still and beautifully clear water. He suddenly laid the flute down and told us stories of the Indians that "long ago" had lived about Walden and Concord; delighting us with simple, clear explanations of the wonders of Walden woods. Again he interrupted himself suddenly, speaking of the various kinds of lilies growing about Walden and calling the wood lilies stately wild things. . . . Upon our return to the shore he helped us gather . . . flowers and laden with many sweet blossoms, we wended our way homeward, rejoicing . . .

Thoreau's way with wildlife continually astonished his visitors. Mrs. Edwin Bigelow once said of him: "Henry would tell all to sit absolutely quiet and close together—then he would go forward cautiously, sprinkle crumbs before them and then retreating, seat himself a little before the others and begin a sort of rolling or humming sound and so would draw squirrels to come and eat at last out of his hands."

The favorite of all Thoreau's wild pets was a mouse, which he said had a nest under his house and came while he ate lunch to pick the crumbs at his feet. It had never seen the race of man before, and therefore became familiar so much the sooner. It ran over his shoes and up the inside of his pant leg, clinging to his flesh with its sharp claws. When he held out a piece of cheese, it came and nibbled between his fingers, and then cleaned its face and paws like a fly. Like the Pied Piper, Thoreau could summon the mouse out of hiding with his flute and display it to his friends. One of the few decorations he permitted in his cabin was a drawing, made on the closet door, of himself and his pet mouse.

For the sake of science Thoreau was willing, occasionally, to sacrifice a specimen or two. Louis Agassiz, who had arrived in Boston from across the Atlantic in the fall of 1846, was anxious to catalogue the flora and fauna of America. James Elliot Cabot enlisted Thoreau's aid, and in the spring of 1847, Thoreau shipped some specimens in to Agassiz's laboratory. Among them, Agassiz found a number of new species including bream, smelt, and shiners. Thoreau also offered to put the hunters and trappers of Concord to work collecting snapping turtles if Agassiz would pay seventy-five cents to a dollar apiece for them. But that offer was not accepted.

Occasionally whole groups of Thoreau's friends came out together to the pond and swarmed into his little cabin. It became quite the fashion to hold picnics on his doorstep, and when it rained, as many as twenty-five or thirty people took refuge inside the tiny cabin. On August 1, 1846, the Woman's Anti-Slavery Society of the town came to the cabin for the annual commemoration of the freeing of the West Indian slaves, and Emerson, W. H. Channing, and Reverend Caleb Stetson spoke to the assembled group.

The only guests that Thoreau did not welcome were the curious—and there were plenty of them—who used any excuse to see the inside of the cabin. When they asked for a glass of water, Thoreau, knowing their real intent, would point to the pond and offer to lend them his dipper. Once two young ladies thus borrowed his dipper and failed to return it, and he fumed in his *Journal:* "I had a right to suppose they came to steal. They were a disgrace to their sex and to humanity. . . . They will never know peace till they have returned the dipper. In all worlds this is decreed."

But despite the visitors, despite all the trips to Concord village and to his parents' home, despite his surveying and fence building and carpentry, and despite the hours devoted to writing, it must not be forgotten that the experiment at Walden was primarily a period of solitude and of communion with nature for Thoreau. It was a period of observing the loons and geese on the pond, the foxes and hawks in the woods, the woodchucks and meadow larks in the fields, the stars and the clouds overhead, the ants and the grasses underfoot, the

flowers and trees all around. And his contemplation was one akin to religious devotion. Frank Sanborn once told Thoreau that when he first moved to Concord in 1855, he was told there were three religious societies in town—the Unitarian, the Orthodox, and the Walden Pond Society. The latter consisted of those who spent their Sunday mornings out walking around Walden Pond enjoying the beauties of nature. Thoreau was unquestionably the high priest of that sect and spent a good part of each day in his devotions.

Although he was never to change the basic pattern of the life he adopted at Walden Pond, by 1847 Thoreau began to feel that he had exhausted the particular benefits of his life there. He had fulfilled his original purpose in coming to the pond—not only had he completed the manuscript of *A Week on the Concord and Merrimack Rivers*, but he had written the first draft of *Walden*. It was time to turn to other fields, he thought, before he got into a rut.

In May, learning of Thoreau's restlessness, Emerson wrote to his brother-in-law, Dr. Charles T. Jackson, urging that Thoreau be included as an assistant on a government geological survey to be made in Michigan. Thoreau would have been admirably suited for the position and wanted very much to go along, but the appointments proved to be political plums over which Jackson had no control and the opportunity was lost.

Then in the late summer of 1847 Emerson himself decided to go abroad for the winter for a lecture tour arranged by his English friends. Mrs. Emerson was in poor health, and the children were too young to travel. Emerson was worried about leaving them alone, but she quickly proposed a solution, suggesting that Thoreau be invited to join them for the winter. His presence would not inconvenience them in the least, for he required no ceremony, and it would assure her husband that his family had the protection and assistance he felt they needed. Emerson quickly agreed to her suggestion, and Thoreau readily accepted their joint invitation.

*A*nd so it was that Thoreau left the pond, on September 6, 1847, exactly two years, two months, and two days after he had moved in. He explained in the pages of *Walden*, "I left the woods for as good a reason as I went there. Perhaps it seemed to me that I had several more lives to live, and could not spare any more time for that one." But in the confidence of his *Journal* he later confessed, "Why I left the woods I do not think I can tell. I have often wished myself back. I do not know any better how I ever came to go there. Perhaps it is none of my business, even if it is yours. Perhaps I wanted a change. There was a little stagnation, it may be. . . . Perhaps if I lived there much longer, I might live there forever. One would think twice befor he accepted heaven on such terms."

Walter Harding, who is Secretary of The Thoreau Society, has edited or been the author of some fifteen books about Thoreau. Mr. Harding's book entitled Thoreau: Man of Concord *was published in 1960.*

The Original Philistines

Photographs by BEN KORNGOLD

The four primitive figurines shown opposite and at right, all more than twenty-five centuries old, were resurrected on the site of Ashdod, the first large Philistine city to be uncovered by archaeologists. Excavations there have yielded a wealth of evidence about early Canaan and about the ancient Philistines, that bellicose people who smite and are smitten on page after page of the Old Testament, and whose carcasses young David promised to feed "unto the fowls of the air, and to the wild beasts of the earth; that all the earth may know that there is a God in Israel."

Ashdod, which lies a few miles inland from the Mediterranean coast of Israel, has been under excavation since 1962 by the Pittsburgh Theological Seminary, the Carnegie Museum in Pittsburgh, and the Israeli Department of Antiquities, represented respectively by Dr. David N. Freedman, Dr. James L. Swauger, and Dr. Moshe Dothan. Last season their discoveries included the skull at right —more likely to have belonged to an indigenous Canaanite than to a Philistine—and a temple shrine containing the figurines. The ram's head opposite was once the spout of a libation bowl. The goddess with the deep cleavage is Astarte, the Venus of the ancient Near East. The head of a man who looks like an ancestor of Charles de Gaulle was once attached to an offering table. Below "de Gaulle" is the head of a round-faced woman smiling enigmatically. These objects represent local deities whom the conquering Philistines adopted, as they did their chief god, Dagon, whose temple at Gaza the blind Samson later pulled down.

No one knows exactly when the Philistines came to Canaan, but there is good evidence that they might have emigrated from Crete by way of Egypt. Once in Canaan, they took possession of the five coastal cities of Ashdod, Ashkelon, Gaza, Ekron, and Gath, probably before 1150 B.C. The first Biblical mention of them occurs in the twenty-first chapter of Genesis, where we learn that Abraham and the Philistine "Abimelech"—the word means "the father is king"—made a covenant of peace. After their Egyptian bondage and the Exodus to the promised land, the children of Israel engaged in continual warfare with the Philistines, as is recorded in the books of Judges, Samuel, and Chronicles. The Bible's final statement about the Philistines is found in Zechariah, the next-to-last book of the Old Testament, and it is a bitter curse: "And a bastard shall dwell in Ashdod, and I will cut off the pride of the Philistines."

In battle the Philistines had two enormous advantages over the factious Israelites: their unity, and the fact that they knew how to forge iron weapons. The Battle of Ebenezer, about 1050 B.C., marked a low point for the ancient Israelites; the Philistines routed them and carried away their sacred Ark of the Law to Ashdod. After that catastrophe, the Israelites at last united under Saul; his successor David drove the Philistines back into coastal territory.

Eventually, when the Assyrians marched into Palestine, both Philistine and Israelite fell before them. Later, Ashdod was captured by the Babylonians, and the current excavations show that they were followed by the Persians, the Greeks, the Romans, the Byzantines, and finally the Arabs. With this last invasion Ashdod ceased to be a city, and the sand swallowed it up. Today, however, a new Ashdod has risen not far from the old one. It will be a seaport for Israel, a few miles south of Tel Aviv.

Opposite: Effigy of a ram's head, superimposed on the ruins of Ashdod.
Right, top to bottom: A skull from the ninth century B.C., a terra-cotta love goddess, a male head from a statuette, and a smiling female head.

HAY
DE TODO
IN
THE PRADO

By HONOR TRACY

Velázquez: *The Adoration of the Ma[gi]*

One of the finest collections of paintings in Europe is housed in a pink-and-fawn-colored building set among grassy banks and green trees, with the spires of San Jerónimo el Real rising above it in the background. The exterior of the Prado is simple, homely, and faintly comic. Its façade is enlivened by a row of plump ladies in grimy stone, denoting Magnificence, Fertility, Admiration, Power, Fame, and other such symbols of euphoria. Inside, time goes at a pace of its own as if dissociating itself from time in the rest of Madrid. The doors seem barely to have opened when the attendants with their own peculiar glee begin to rattle their keys and drape the postcard stands. That is to say, those attendants who are in the great old tradition and either ignore visitors until the moment they can be turned out or treat them as potential felons. A truly dedicated follower of this tradition, standing within a few yards of the Lady of Elche, will have it that no such work has ever existed. It all goes together with bristly chins and garlicky breath and ankle-length overcoats and, like many ancient institutions today, is threatened by newly emerging forces. A race is springing up who not only know what their museum contains and where to find it but are willing and even eager to share their knowledge.

For years I have been intending to work methodically through the collection, but invariably stick in the Spanish rooms. These become ever more absorbing with familiarity, for every Spanish quality is here in one form or another—the extravagance, the earthiness, the harshness, the illusion and disillusion, the gay and grotesque, the humming *muchedumbre* of bees in the Spanish bonnet. The themes are God and Man, nature getting a bare look in. Landscape is used as a setting only, usually in the form of a park or a purely conventional line of hills or trees. Even as rural a picture as *Los Borrachos* was painted in Velázquez's studio and the low foothills of the Guadarramas put in from memory. Perhaps the very grandeur of the country itself has something to do with it, perhaps the material is too intractable, too wild and stubborn and on too vast a scale to compose, glaring under too harsh a light. Whatever the reason, a Spanish Constable or Monet or Van Gogh is somehow unthinkable.

The religious painting faithfully expresses the national temper-

ament, that is to say, it is inspired more easily by the Crucifixion, the Virgin weeping below the Cross, the martyrdoms of saints and apostles, by bones, skulls, flagellations, and the torments of hell than by the Joyful Mysteries. Good Friday rather than Easter is the day for the Christians of Spain. What a feeling of personal grief there is at the hour of Christ's death! not only in the churches where among the swathed images, empty fonts, and extinguished lamps crowds kneel in adoration of the Host, which, enthroned in a bank of flowers and candles, is the one sign of hope left in an almost brutal desolation, but in the streets and houses as well. Flags fly at half-mast, people go in mourning, voices are kept low, even to chuckle in a public place is to invite reproachful looks. It is as if all these stoic, pent-up men and women had saved their private tears to add them once in the year to a universal flood. Easter is a different story: it is something of an anticlimax; there is the Easter duty to perform, processions to watch, then probably a family luncheon, a *corrida* in the afternoon, and fireworks at night. It is *fiesta,* even *gran fiesta,* but it does not move the people in the way that Good Friday does, nor is there the burst of joy in the air that is felt on Easter Day in Greek or Russian Orthodox churches.

So, then, it is the human rather than the divine side of Christ's nature and life that the Spanish painter is drawn to, and those artists who excel in the human sphere appear to me to do so in the religious. It may be a quirk of taste, but the religious works of Velázquez and Zurbarán, even of Goya, move me more than those of El Greco or Murillo, perhaps by their down-to-earth quality. If we go right up to *La Adoracíon de los Reyes,* we see a Virgin with a dull peasant face holding a Child who looks all too sharp and knowing, a future cacique you might think, while He receives the homage of three clodhoppers. If we stand a little way off, the picture exudes reverence, tranquillity, and love, all through a simple but magic use of light and shade. Beside the matter-of-fact presentations of Velázquez, the "spirituality" of an El Greco subject with the anemic face, the upturned eyes, and the spiky mole's hands seems trite.

To the portrayal of human beings the great Spanish artists

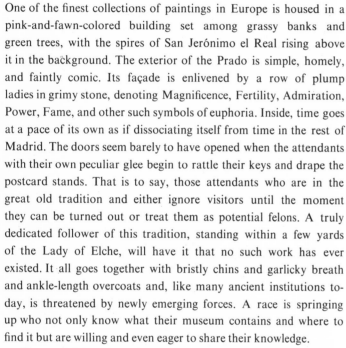

Goya: *The Family of Charles IV*   Velázquez: *The Infanta Doña Margarita*

bring all the raciness and observation and irony that pervade Spanish literature. Truth comes first, without regard to power or place, let alone to compassion or chivalry. What court painter but a Spanish one would risk showing his king as a red-faced bumpkin and his queen as the very pattern of misguided vanity, with lasciviously sparkling button eyes, a flat nose, and thin lips compressed to hide the missing teeth? Such indeed were that catastrophic pair, Carlos IV and Maria Luisa, by all contemporary accounts, and it seems not to have occurred to Goya to depict them in any other way. Nor, for that matter, do we hear that they were anything but delighted with his performance.

There is the portrait by Velázquez of the Infanta Margarita, small hands firm on the huge frothing and shimmering skirt of red and silver, the curls shining, the wide confident eyes incuriously fixed on their great delineator, the Hapsburg cheek bulging a little as if over a lollipop, the Hapsburg nose already bulbing, the Hapsburg arrogance none too far away, all in a marvelously suspended animation. The Venerable Mother Jerónima de la Fuente, grasping her crucifix as other women grasp an axe, reminds us of every shrewd, hard, patient old Spanish nun we have ever seen. When Velázquez painted her, she was waiting in Seville to take ship for Manila to found the convent of Santa Clara there; but we may still run across her at any time, marshaling her orphans along a dusty road, resolutely extracting alms from people in cafés, totting up the accounts of her convent, telling her beads in a come-no-nonsense manner on the wooden seat of a crowded and appalling train, a creature not of today, tomorrow, or yesterday but of always, a drab brown figure expressive not only of the woman but of her land and her Church, painted when Velázquez was twenty-one.

The famous dwarfs, or *bufones,* stand in a row: Don Diego de Acedo, a court official and not a jester at all, who set up to be the painter's cousin and a man of letters, a tiny creature in black with a hat far too big, and cocked at an angle of defiance, who holds a book half the size of his body and who is fairly swelling with a secret importance, all against a background of wintry chaos; Don Sebastián de Morra, jester to the Prince Cardinal in the Low

Countries, who fancied himself as traveler and man of the world; the idiot boy from Vallecas, Lezcano, said to have been born with all his teeth, here vacantly staring and holding some cards in his feeble little hands, used as the butt and recreation of young Prince Baltasar Carlos; and then Calabacillas, or Little Pumpkins, of imbecile appearance but with a turn of wit that Philip IV relished. All of them, in the nakedness of their despair and of their futile attempts to escape, have the power to excite horror and arouse compassion in us centuries after the ending of their short and luckless lives, and all may be seen any day in the flesh hawking their lottery tickets in the street or at any church door.

I seldom go through these rooms, where one masterpiece follows the other in a dazzling array, without thinking of the King's obstinate endeavors to make a hidalgo of Velázquez. No pains were spared, no euphemisms shirked, points were stretched to the point of bursting: wearisome research went on to prove the painter a man of pure Spanish blood, free from the Jewish or Moorish taint, a descendant of people who never had traded or served, an artist who painted by his sovereign's order or to please himself, and never for vile money. All this was to make him acceptable to the Noble Order of Santiago, for which he was repeatedly proposed by Philip IV and as often rejected by the Order, with an obduracy which was no less rigid than the King's and which provides a remarkable footnote to Spanish absolutism. One can understand the attitude of the King, for rank seems all-important to those who have it and little beyond, but how to explain that of the artist? To be Velázquez, and to yearn to be "Don Diego"! Behold, what a piece of work is a man.

Now and again when receptivity weakens, it is a capital thing to sit down and observe the human scene. Every time I go in, I recognize certain individuals of cultured appearance and aspect mild and vague who, I believe, have made the building their permanent home. They have the look of people who never go out, and one suspects that were they ever to do so they would be run over almost at once. In here they move purposefully and with assurance from one canvas to the next, and their comments, if any, are brief and to the point:

Velázquez: *The Venerable Mother Jerónima*   Velázquez: *The Buffoons Diego de Acedo, Sebastián de Morra, Francisco Lezcano, and Calabacillas*

they seem unaware rather than scornful of the philistines around them who are commenting in a blithe lowbrow way that Don Carlos is the image of Onkel Ignaz, *nicht?* or that the *Maja Desnuda* will catch her death and serve the hussy right; and they look so hungrily at a painting it seems as if their eyes will draw the color out.

These are a peculiar species of fauna, not painters themselves but experts on the matter of painting. They know everything except how to do it; ask them a question concerning dates, attributions, influences, and they will rap out the answer like a machine telling your weight. Another Prado species worthy of note is the copyist, who provides us with material for long, if fruitless, speculation. Why has the lady with the bobbed white hair and the blouse of one blue and the skirt of another picked *Los Borrachos* for her model? She inhabits a little world of cheap pensions and valiant doing-without: what has she to do with Velázquez's ribald old topers, with Bacchus of the sly smooth face and vine-wreathed head egging them on, a young smart aleck making a fool of elders and betters? She screws up her fierce little virgin's face and glares at the glorious sunlit abandon before her, then rapidly puts in a stroke or two of the brush and steps back to admire the effect. Steal a glance at her work and the mystery deepens. Were it not for the plump white torso of Bacchus and the ruby glow on the peasant's features, one would hardly guess what it was intended to be.

The young man who copies Goya's *Maja Desnuda* has a more promising air. Someone or other copies it every day, but this poor young man has Artist written all over him. He must be a genius, with his wild eyes and hollow cheeks and the little fringe of despondent beard. The cotton trousers are dirty and torn, and toes poke out of the rope-soled shoes. It is plain that he denies himself everything to buy paints and brushes and canvas. Now and again he fervently rumples his long black hair. With lively anticipation we peep over his shoulder and *caramba!* what do we see? Goya's exquisite line and delicate luminous flesh has turned into a mauvish lump of meat. But the young man works away with the same dedication and forgetfulness of self as the little old lady in blue, and as the wan individual in the smock and velvet beret who seems to have

wandered out of *La Vie de Bohème,* and as the scowling fellow with the head and shoulders of a picador.

I must describe the harrowing experience of one morning, very early, so early that I had achieved the universal ambition and got *Las Meninas* to myself. There I stood, half expecting one of the miraculous figures to give a sign of life: Maribárbola perhaps, who from the look on her broad dwarf's face seemed on the verge of passing some remark about me, something sharp and disagreeable and witty, to make the little Infanta and her ladies burst out laughing; or the mastiff, who after three centuries might suddenly lose patience and turn to snap at Nicolasito de Pertusato's foot as it dug him in the flank; or Velázquez himself, who might call out to bystanders to go away before they spoiled the composition of the group. It is difficult to contemplate this stupendous picture without bursting into cliché, as we see from the ejaculations of notables listed in the *catalogue raisonné,* including the "What! are they still alive?" of that naughty old fraud, the Countess d'Aulnoy, who never saw it at all. I gazed and gazed, feeling all the satisfaction tinged with melancholy that great art gives and hoping no one would come just yet, for one could stand there by the hour and never be tired of it.

At this moment a woman, blonde and stringy and with bright hypnotic eyes, approached and in Germanic accents revealed that the painting was thought by many to be Velázquez's masterpiece. She gave an account of it and of the figures included, with dates and biographical matter, and drew attention to many felicities that without her aid I must undoubtedly have overlooked. She hunted me hither and yon to study it the better from this angle and that, she explained that the mirrors were put there because the picture seen thus at one remove came more magically alive than ever and forced me to try them and confirm that it was so. This fiend, it is perhaps worth remarking, looked for no reward: it merely had not crossed her mind that anyone else could know anything, and she was urged on by an appalling lust for communication.

One swallow does not make a summer, and accordingly I hesitate to classify this scourge among the Prado species: yet when at last she roamed away in search of fresh woods and pastures new

44

Velázquez: *The Drinkers*

Velázquez: *The Maids of Honor*

Carreño: *The Monster Nude and Clothed*

and the room filled up with a herd of young ladies from some good convent, it struck me that I had undergone that same experience before, in that very same place and with that same terrible lady or one exactly like her. Did then a species exist? or was she but the Phantom of the Prado? I will probably never know, but I can never approach the Maids of Honor now without throwing uneasy glances round me.

The human spectacle is one of never failing interest and amusement, with every now and then a little chink appearing in the wall of bodies so that we may catch a glimpse of a painting. There are the great crowds of foreigners, whose faces have turned the color of boiled shrimps in the sun and who seem on the point of expiring with heat. Rich old American ladies in teen-ager hats seem to preponderate, growling to each other over the souvenir stands in hoarse manly voices; Germans frown at the catalogue as if to warn it they will stand none of its nonsense; French ask the way to the *salas francesas* before anything else; English move briskly as if taking the dog for a walk; and there are Asians, Indians, Africans, people from all over the world who, however, tend in the presence of Art to divide into three main groups—the reverent, the truculent, and the facetious. Spaniards are noticeably in a minority, and apart from priests, nuns, and their little charges, very often the only ones in sight are couples on their honeymoon, this being a moment of life when the Spanish are apt to improve their minds once and for all, so that they need never tinker with them again.

I know several educated *madrileños* who have never been in the Prado at all. One of these, a woman, is nevertheless very fond of talking about it, and whenever we meet, she buttonholes me for news of Goya, Velázquez, Murillo, and the other great ones. I must describe it all to her, room by room, as to one without the gift of sight or movement. She is particularly interested in the two singular paintings by Carreño, *La Monstrua Desnuda* and *La Monstrua Vestida*, which show a little girl of repulsive fatness, like some little American darling bloated with ice cream, pie, and love, first naked and then richly clothed. We discuss them interminably, speculating as to who the original can be and why anyone, whether patron or

artist, should have desired to fix her loathsome form in perpetuity.

"I should so like to see them!"

My friend always accompanies these words with a sigh of longing. In a like, wistful manner I have heard people along the Demerara coast speak of "the interior," the deep primeval Amazonian forest. For them, however, it would have meant an expedition of days or weeks, with Indians, mosquitoes, kibouri, snakes, and probably fever. My friend has only to leave her flat, turn to the right, and right again, and walk straight on until she comes to the Prado doors: seventeen minutes in all, four or five in a taxi.

"If only I could see them!"

She is, of course, an extreme case.

One could really move into the Prado and spend the rest of one's life there. *Hay de todo*, except baths. In a charming open yard with green shrubs a friendly waitress will serve you mysterious snacks, from combination dishes with "potatoes cheeps" to "spilt banane." Here, too, the human element adds greatly to the pleasure. One noon there was a fat red smiling man from Lancashire, his shirt open to reveal a furry chest and tummy, sipping a glass of champagne while the bottle lolled in the cooler beside it. No doubt the honest fellow was celebrating his first encounter with the world of art, and I was much edified to think of the opportunities for mental enrichment that the affluent society offers to all. But when I returned to the cantina just before it closed, there he still was, a little rosier, smiling more widely, high living and low thinking, with various dead bottles lying around him, a curious phenomenon indeed in that frugal *ambiance*. The waitress looked on him with indulgence, as if to say that if he wanted to do his drinking there, so he might. And when you come down to it, he was but killing two birds with one stone, for no one could ever say that he had not been to the Prado. I suspect, too, that he was the only man in the room or even the building that Velázquez or Goya would have considered worth painting.

There is seldom a dull moment in the Prado.

Honor Tracy is a journalist, essayist, and novelist whose most recent novel, The First Day of Friday, *appeared in 1963. This essay is taken from* Spanish Leaves, *to be published in October by Random House.*

One might have thought that the last story about Oscar Wilde had been told, that the last *chronique scandaleuse* had been dragged from the remotest volume of memoirs, and that the brains of every ancient Parisian concierge had been picked in the hope that in his guttersnipe days he might have been offered a glass of absinthe by the notorious M. Sebastian Melmoth, as Wilde was then calling himself.

But there is one story that has never been told, and I shall tell it here. And though it could be narrated in a very few words, that is not how I propose to go about it.

Besides, the story needs an introduction.

The scene was the bedroom of a rambling Victorian house in Torquay. I was going on fifteen and I had been rudely awakened from an innocent sleep, in the small hours of the morning, by a burly man with a thick black mustache. My father. He strode over to the window and tore back the curtain with a simple gesture. Then he sat down at my desk and began to write.

I rubbed my eyes and blinked at him with some astonishment. He was evidently in a towering rage—but about what? I knew better than to ask, and waited till he had finished. After a few moments he threw down his pencil, rose to his feet, and glared at me as though I were something unclean.

He pointed to the desk with a trembling finger. "That," he shouted, "is what That Man did." With which he stalked from the room, slamming the door behind him.

I was still scarcely awake, but I slid out of bed and took up the paper on which he had written, in block capitals, this macabre message: ILLUM CRIMEN HORRIBILE QUÓD NON NOMI-NANDUM EST, "that horrible crime which is not to be named."

Then it all came back in a flood of humiliating memory—the violent scene of the night before, my mother's tears, and the flames creeping round my beautiful book, the book bound in white parchment powdered with silver fleurs-de-lis, the book that Reggie had given me, *The Picture of Dorian Gray.*

Reggie was a neighbor of ours, in his early thirties. He was rich, volatile, and extremely popular with the old ladies who formed the majority of Torquay's population. Nowadays, his walk, his clothes, the sinuous gestures of his delicately manicured hands, would have made it screamingly obvious to everybody that he was a homosexual. But Torquay was still sunk deep in the dark ages, as far as *that* sort of thing was concerned. Never for a moment did it occur to anybody that his mannerisms might be more than amiable eccentricities. "Dear Reggie is so artistic," murmured the dowagers, as they sipped their tea in his elegant drawing room. Even when he came to lunch at our house with his cheeks heavily rouged, my mother was merely amused. "Dear Reggie has actually begun to 'touch up,'" she observed to my father. "I wonder whatever he will do next?"

What he did next was to give me *The Picture of Dorian Gray.*

I was a good-looking boy—at this distance of time one may be pardoned for mentioning it—but I was also a strangely innocent one. On the evenings when I went to dine with him, which always ended with music, I sometimes wished that he would not breathe so heavily down the back of my neck when I was playing Chopin, but I suspected nothing sinister. The only thing that disturbed me, ever so faintly, was his apparent anxiety to make me drunk. At the age of fifteen a little Médoc and a glass of vintage port are enough to produce a considerable exhilaration, but at these dinners, when we were served by a young Greek footman who might have posed for Praxiteles, there was always champagne, and Armagnac, and an assortment of liqueurs as colorful as the celebrated passage about the jewels in *Dorian Gray.*

The present of *Dorian Gray,* which arrived on the morning of my fifteenth birthday, was presumably intended to produce another form of intoxication, and in this it certainly succeeded. As I have already mentioned, it was bound in white parchment powdered with silver fleurs-de-lis, but even if it had been a paperback, I should have fallen under its heady spell. From the moment when the curtain rose on the studio scene, with the scent of lilacs drifting through the open window, I was enthralled. True, some of the epigrams were a little over my head, and sometimes I felt faintly cheated because the author was so very mysterious about what Dorian actually *did* that was so unspeakably wicked. (In my innocence I suspected that it must be something to do with naked women.) But these were minor drawbacks to the sheer enchantment of page after page of purple

By BEVERLEY NICHOLS

prose, as heavily encrusted with jewels as a Fabergé cigarette case. This, I thought, was one of the great masterpieces of all time. Odd as it may seem, I still think so.

All through that long day of April, I pored over *Dorian Gray*, and in the evening my father found me reading it in the garden by the light of the dying sun. His reaction, as we have seen, was swift and brutal. When he hurled the book into the fire, he shouted that he was sending it back to its accursed author, who was burning in the quenchless fires of Hell. And when I dared to ask "Why? What did he *do*?" he could find no words to answer me in the English language.

"Illum crimen horribile . . ."

What has all this to do with our story? Very little, except to date it—and to accentuate the shock it made upon me when at last I heard it.

First the date. That was thirty years later. Incredibly, during those three long decades, the name of Oscar Wilde was never mentioned in our household. Europe might burst into flames—and did; Evil incarnate might stalk abroad—and did; but the author of *The Importance of Being Earnest* represented a sort of Evil beyond Evil. He was the ultimate horror, the Thing.

And then, quite suddenly and casually, my mother mentioned that he had once stayed with her family when she was a girl.

"He stayed with you? Oscar Wilde actually *stayed* with you?"

"I am afraid so."

"Why have you never told me this before?"

The answer was characteristic. "Because if I had known what he was, at the time, I should have run out of the house. I would have rather been in the room with a snake."

But at last she brought herself to speak.

It was in the winter of 1883. Oscar had recently returned from a lecture tour in America where he had been exploited as a sort of brilliant clown. This was the heyday of his aesthetic period, the day of the velvet jacket, the flowing cloak, and the soft felt hat. None of the major works had yet been written; the American dollars were soon spent, and on his return he was obliged to continue lecturing.

His first appearance was booked in that hideous, smoke-blackened center of British industrialism, Leeds.

Now it so happened that on the outskirts of Leeds lived a formidable old lady called Rebecca Shalders, my grandmother. Although she was a model of Victorian propriety, she was evidently keenly interested in the arts, and whenever any celebrities arrived in the city she had a habit of annexing them. As she was rich, hospitable, and not unintelligent, the celebrities were only too happy to be annexed. And they usually sang for their supper.

But Oscar did not sing for his supper. He was far too tired. ("Languid" was my mother's adjective.) Besides, he was extremely cold. The lecture hall had been inadequately heated, the audience none too responsive, and afterward there had been a five-mile drive through the snow in my grandmother's carriage—a drive in which she had probably taken more than her fair share of the rug.

So after a large brandy and soda he had excused himself and made his way up the old oak staircase and taken himself to bed. During this brief interlude he had made only one remark which my mother remembered. "One's only real life," he had said, "is the life one never leads."

"Never mind," said my grandmother when he had gone. "At least we will see that the poor man has a good breakfast."

On the following morning my mother came down early to the dining room, to find the old lady hovering round the solid mahogany sideboard. This was laden with a weight of food which, even in Victorian Yorkshire, might have been regarded as almost ostentatious. Here my mother's recollection becomes crystal clear, maybe because she was later to inherit most of the silver plates and dishes in which it was served. Thus, she vividly recalled the chafing dish filled with grandmother's special kedgeree, the Georgian platters piled with sliced ham, the Regency sauceboat with the pickled cranberries, the Sheffield plate which accommodated the cold grouse, and the cumbersome Victorian device, mounted over a spirit lamp, for the eggs, the bacon, and the sausages. At various times in my life I too have been served from the same dishes. But not all at once.

Oscar was very late. More butter had to be spread on the kedgeree, and there was a fear that the spirit lamp might run dry. But at last he made his appearance. He was still wearing his fur coat, and my mother, with a curious flicker of memory (I was a tireless cross-examiner!), recalled that the collar was still damp from the snow of the night before, and that she had thought that the fur must be dyed and not "good." And he looked paler and more languid than ever.

"And now Mr. Wilde," said my grandmother, "what would you like to begin with?"

Slowly he surveyed the sideboard, and a faint but perceptible shudder agitated his body, which even in those days was beginning to run to fat. For a moment he stood there in silence. Then he walked over to the window and looked out onto the cheerless landscape. The standard roses were muffled in straw, and in the distance the lake was a sheet of sullen glass.

He spoke very softly.

"I should like," he said, "some raspberries."

My grandmother felt that she could not have heard aright.

"I beg your pardon, Mr. Wilde?"

He turned and smiled.

He spoke even more softly, as though, in this incongruous atmosphere, at this unpropitious hour, a prose poem were forming in his willful brain.

"Some *pale yellow* raspberries," he said.

And that is the end of the story.

"Story," did I say? How can one make a story from a single word? That is a question I would not venture to answer. For after all, it was not I who said the word, but Oscar. He had a way with words.

Among his many novels, plays, and essays, Beverley Nichols's best-known work may be Laughter on the Stairs, *a book on gardening.*

of the metes and bounds of tribal lands, of the proper ritual for community celebrations.) The oral histories are often astonishingly long—in Uganda they encompass the reigns of more than thirty kings—and they are rich in significant detail for the social historian. But they are completely encapsulated. Their chronology is local, without a casual cross reference to external cultures. Only an occasional reference to eclipse or earthquake offers some chance of calibrating the local sequence of events with those of the world outside.

Nevertheless, the African historians hope to push the written record back at least to the opening of the sixteenth century by using these oral traditions. It will require a staggering amount of work on their part. Hundreds, even thousands, of village historians must be interviewed. The tapes must be transcribed, then translated from the dialect into French or English—the two languages of scholarship in sub-Sahara Africa. Only then can these local histories be interpreted, analyzed, and recast in modern form. The capstone of this colossal task of compiling a history of all Africa which will be comparable in scope and accuracy to Western historiography will probably be the *Encyclopedia Africana*. This project, begun under the editorship of the late, great Afro-American W. E. B. Dubois, is now under way in Ghana.

For the historian of art and architecture, the problem is also difficult. The durability of the art forms of the African past depends on the material out of which they are fabricated and the climate in which they occur. The mud architecture of the dry Saharan regions lasts almost indefinitely—a peasant's hut may collect the dust of centuries. And fragile funeral wreaths of herbs and flowers survive in Egyptian tombs for millennia. But in equatorial Africa, heat, humidity, bacteria, and insects combine to limit the life of all organic materials —for example, wood, fabric, and leather—to a few decades. Thus even monumental architecture and sculpture is tragically short-lived. How great is the loss caused by this equatorial attrition can be clearly seen in the magnificent fragments which survive in the museums of Ghana, Nigeria, and Uganda. From the great bronze-incrusted doors and portrait sculpture of Benin and Ife we get a glimpse of a splendid plastic tradition. But these metal masterpieces constitute only rare landmarks in the vast terra incognita of African art. The voids in between must be filled in by patient research on the part of historian, archaeologist, and ethnographer—an immense task that is scarcely under way. And here, as in social historiography, isolation from the main world currents imposes certain limitations. Because of them, the African art histories are apt to be more typological than chronological.

In architecture the problem is somewhat easier. Because of climate the Saharan mud architecture and the wood and stone architecture of the Ethiopian highlands survive fairly well. And this is very fortunate, for these areas afford some of the most beautiful as well as the most functional folk architec-

New museum, Accra, Ghana

Aging modern tribal masks for tourist market, Ivory Coast

"Airport art" on souvenir stand, Abidjan, Ivory Coast

Young painter and art dealer, Lagos, Nigeria

Bas-relief on skyscraper, Lagos

European-educated artist showing masks of his own design, Ibadan, Nigeria

tures of the world. Equatorial Africa also abounds in an astonishing and beautiful variety of architectural forms, but they are highly transient. Even the great royal tombs of Uganda are built entirely of straw (including the arch ribs which support the thatched roofs) and must be reconstructed every twenty years.

Since this vegetable-fiber architecture is so well adapted to the tropical climate, and since the raw materials are cheap and plentiful, one would expect to find a great demand in present-day Africa for modern chemicals that would render these fibers resistant to flame, rot, and vermin. But it is a typical African paradox that, instead, thatch is everywhere being replaced by corrugated metal. Made of either galvanized steel or (increasingly) aluminum, these shiny new roofs wink up at one's plane all across the continent. Expensive, ugly, and hellishly hot, they nevertheless have the prestige of modernity. They are longer-lived and more trouble-free than the traditional thatch, and they mark the owner as up-to-date. Thus do climate and technology, either singly or in combination, work to obliterate the wonderful folk architectures of Africa.

This high mortality rate of the artifacts of material culture is one reason for the visual poverty of the average village. To the casual visitor from the West there is a startling lack of that magnificent religious and funerary art which he has seen in the museums. Even the simplest tools, utensils, and furniture of daily life seem nonexistent. But the ethnographer will explain that appearances are somewhat deceptive here, and that the lack of visual art forms is more than made up for by a wealth of poetry, song, and dance. Normally inaccessible to the outsider, this is the chief vehicle of African creativity.

But these "invisible" forms of art are not immune to civilization, either, and will require protection if they are to survive. Radio penetrates everywhere. Cheap tabloids follow literacy. The shoddiest of all movies (mostly American, alas!) dominate the motion-picture screens of the towns. Patriotic Africans are much disturbed by this cultural erosion. In both Nigeria and Ghana I heard concern expressed about the vulgarizing impact of Afro-American jazz upon indigenous music. Even so careful an artist as the American dancer Pearl Primus, who has the greatest respect for African dancing and makes a serious attempt to interpret it, was viewed with dismay. Her so-called "ethnic" dances were felt in Ghana to be inaccurate, inartistic, non-African.

The poets and novelists face another sort of problem. Generally speaking they aspire to write on African themes for a mass African audience. But that audience scarcely exists as yet—the illiterate herdsmen and peasants are still the captives of the oral tradition. Hence the paradoxical situation in which African writing is better known in Paris or London than in the author's own country. This creates an ambivalence of which the writers are uncomfortably aware. They are confident that a pan-African audience will emerge; meanwhile, they have to act as though it already exists.

With independence, the people of some thirty-six African states have stepped through the looking glass. Issues which were literally matters of life and death before liberation seem now to have evaporated. Even in Algeria and Kenya, where the battle for independence assumed murderous dimensions, one hears little talk of those days and sees little evidence of them. In Nairobi, where only eight years ago the white planters wore side arms in the main streets and the natives were herded into "protective" villages, the visitor today sees both sides placidly riding the same busses, drinking in the same bars, attending the same schools. The traumatic experiences of the past undoubtedly left wounds, but these appear to be healing with astonishing rapidity. Instead, a whole new range of problems now becomes apparent. Having won that so-desired future, the new countries suddenly discover an unexpected importance in the past. As long as they were colonial pawns the prestige of Western culture held unchallenged ascendancy. In the colonialist capitals the small African elite modeled its life after Western prototypes (importing canned American goods, for instance, or performing Noel Coward comedies in their amateur theatricals). But, with independence, a profound shift in taste has set in. All over Africa today new idioms in dress, décor, cuisine, and protocol are being evolved before one's eyes.

Nowhere is this clearer than in matters of dress—a problem complicated by the fact that in large areas of the continent clothing is a very new idea indeed. Thus one reads in a Ghanaian newspaper an angry letter from an upcountry reader who writes to denounce (in good English) the statement of another reader who has said that maidens still appear naked in the market of his natal village; they do so no longer, he indignantly declares. In the very same paper there are pictures of local fashion shows and beauty contests in the Western style.

Businessmen and government officials often wear Western-style suits. The light-weight, drip-dry suit is ubiquitous. (But it is always dark in color, never white: the immaculate white linen suit of the Empire seems to have vanished along with the colonialists who wore them.) A high government official in Addis Ababa, or a college professor in Ibadan, may dress very much like his opposite number in Rome or London. But all over Africa the male can apparently wear either local or international dress with equal aplomb, changing his costume —and thereby his whole appearance—with enviable ease. Side by side with the internationalist fashion, national costumes are often *de rigueur* for formal occasions. Thus in Ghana and Nigeria a capacious full-sleeved, knee-length tunic is worn over tight trousers of matching material; alternately, a great toga is wrapped around the waist and thrown over the shoulder, Roman style. The material is cotton, either

Mud Hut to Skyscraper

One-family compound of thatched huts, northern Togo

Huts with corrugated iron roofs, Uganda

New suburbs of Accra, Ghana

MARC RIBOUD—MAGNUM

Air-conditioned motel, northern Cameroon

MARC RIBOUD—MAGNUM

Cool mud houses, Kano, Nigeria

Twenty-five-story government building, Lagos, Nigeria

white or boldly patterned in brilliant colors. In Ghana the formal-dress version of this costume is made up in the traditional *kente* cloth—an expensive, hand-woven fabric of multicolored six-inch-wide strips, woven on a narrow loom and then stitched together. In the Sudan the classic white burnoose is worn by all classes of men, at all types of work. It is topped off with a turban of white-and-green or white-and-orange cotton.

The same sort of inventiveness may be found in women's clothes. In Ethiopian cities there is an almost universal costume—a very long, very full skirt over which is worn a long sari-like scarf. Both are always made of a sheer, hand-woven white cotton with multicolored borders. Essentially this same dress is worn by working-class women in daytime and—more stylishly cut and carefully made—by upper-class women at evening parties. In both cases it is extremely becoming to the chiseled features, dark coloring, and slight figures of the Ethiopian women. It is so popular that very little Western-style dress is seen on the streets.

Not only clothing but woven fabrics themselves are relatively recent arrivals in equatorial Africa. The only truly indigenous fabric seems to be tapa cloth, which is beaten out of various tree barks. And even today very little cloth is actually produced in Africa—most of it being imported from England, Switzerland, and the Orient. In view of this the control that African consumers exert over the patterns and colors of these fabrics is simply astonishing. Almost without exception they are ravishingly becoming to African pigmentation, physique, and temperament. In Kenya and Uganda one sees flaming yellows, reds, oranges, and umbers in bold, large-scaled patterns. In contrast the Ethiopian taste seems cool and reserved: a favorite import seems to be diaphanous nylon scarves in fluorescent pinks, greens, and tangerine. In Nigeria grayed blues, muted violets, and sulphureous yellow-greens are popular. In Ghana one length of these fabrics forms a skirt, and another forms a sort of hammock where the ubiquitous baby sleeps astride its mother's hips. The fascinating thing about these beautiful costumes is that they are genuinely national and at the same time, "high style" and popular.

His past confronts the African with all sorts of challenges. The re-evaluation of his own folklore was inevitable, since it represents a resource of both cultural and economic value. But its exploitation and development is fraught with great danger for both folk art and folk artist, as many African ministries of culture are well aware. Ethnographers, art historians, and museum curators are exploring this field for the loftiest reasons. But folklore is also a valuable tourist asset (along with scenery and wild animals) because it attracts hard currency to the unbalanced economies of the new countries. How to make use of it without corrupting it is a delicate problem in cultural engineering and one for which there is not much precedent. Thus the commericalization of traditional sculpture is already far advanced. At every airport and every big hotel a curio shop sells inept mass-produced imitations of the masks, idols, and totems of the various tribes. And the European sections of the big cities are crisscrossed with peddlers of "antique" sculptures (occasionally really antique), some of them from half a continent away. No one seems to know exactly how this trade has developed. It obviously shows the presence of alert entrepreneurs (white and black) responding on a local level to a new tourist demand for "curios." And it obviously poses a clear threat to the survival of one of the richest and most varied plastic idioms on earth.

This type of commercial degradation of native traditions is the most apparent, but it is merely symptomatic of the general impact of modern industrial society upon all forms of preindustrial art and artisanship. Even under the best circumstances the results can be unfortunate. In Khartoum I met the Brigadier General who, as director of Sudanese tourism, has been catapulted willy-nilly into a key position in folkloristic activities. A cultured man and a painter of some merit, he had been asked by the government to stage the first national celebration of folk dance and song. Presented at the National Theatre in Khartoum, this brought together dancers from all the ethnic groups in the Republic, from the devout and decorous Moslems of the north to the pagan pastoral peoples of the south. These latter habitually wear no clothes, and the General had felt constrained to dress them, for the plane trip to the capital as well as for the stage. But dress them how? He clothed them in the only garments he had at hand—bras and short skirts for the girls, short pants for the men. The aesthetic impact of this costume on these handsome dancers was grotesque—a fact which the General realized. What to do? He needs skilled designers and choreographers who can study these splendid people in their native habitat. Though they do not wear clothes, they have magnificent ornaments and jewelry; from these, experts could evolve a costume which, while meeting the minimum requirements of modern travel and metropolitan streets, might enhance rather than cripple their appearance. But, as in so many African dilemmas: where to find the experts? the funds? most of all, the *time*?

In Accra I saw a program of song and dance staged by one of the many amateur groups that are an exciting feature of the Ghanaian capital. Initially I found the skill and enthusiasm of these young dancers and musicians engrossing. But long before the program was finished (and despite the different names of the fifteen different dances), it became for my taste very monotonous. The program had no beginning, no end, no sense of theatrical *structure*. One of the ethnographers in the cultural ministry explained this paradox. Under primitive conditions there are no performers and no

Tribesmen on former London bus, Nairobi, Kenya

Modern French hotel, age-old dugout, Abidjan, Ivory Coast

Motor bike on new Champs Elysées, Ouagadougou, Upper Volta

…mir's Cadillac and ceremonial umbrella, northern Nigeria

The pause that refreshes, in Kenya

…upermarket, Lagos, Nigeria

Middle-class living room, Lagos, Nigeria

spectators. Everyone dances and no one gets bored: when one gets tired, one stops. How to restructure these art forms for the modern relationship of artist-proscenium-audience without at the same time extinguishing the fire and spontaneity is a central problem of the African folklorist.

All serious observers realize that the local governments must intervene if all these forms of folk art are to be saved from the certain annihilation which otherwise awaits them. At the same time, it is difficult for these new countries—beset by so many more urgent problems—to give effectual help. Even in the remotest bush the economic base of the village artist-artisan is being radically altered. With the decline of paganism and the spread of secular culture, the demand for ritual and funerary art declines. Traditionally all this art was commissioned piece by piece, and the identity of the artist was usually well known. Robbed of patronage, the artist becomes a simple craftsman. Wood carvers become carpenters or cabinetmakers. Metalworkers become blacksmiths. And the decay of the idiom proceeds at an accelerated pace. Thus, all folklore, traditional arts and crafts, and historic architecture are in a perilous state.

Actually, three interrelated but separate cultural tasks are involved here: (1) the preservation of the artist-artisan; (2) the preservation of his craft or métier; and (3) the preservation, physically, of examples of traditional forms of his art. The ethnographic museum is the proper vehicle for the last. Craft schools and apprenticeship training programs can accomplish the second. But only a comprehensive program for state-subsidized and protected workshops and retail outlets can save the craftsman and attract a new generation. Without help, handicraft production cannot be expected to survive the naked competition of modern mass production.

No African state, so far as I know, has yet been able to launch such a program, though there are many interesting new institutions on The Dark Continent that hope to solve one or another aspect of this problem. A program of training schools, craft shops, and retail outlets is under discussion in Ghana. Ethnographic museums are being created everywhere; they might well take their inspiration from the new Institute of Arab Folklore in Cairo. Soon to be housed on its own new campus near the Pyramids of Giza, this combined museum and research facility will have five sections—painting and sculpture, architecture, dance, music, and literature—and will be the center of a vast projected program for the regeneration of Egyptian folklore and handicrafts.

Many African universities now have advanced institutes for national studies and are carrying on impressive work in music, literature, history, and the visual arts. At the universities of Ife and Ibadan in Nigeria, a group of devoted scholars are working directly with folk artists in the villages, subsidizing their work and displaying and selling it in the cities. Here, too, are the *mbari* (literally, "creation") clubs, aimed at establishing centers of artistic activity in the rapidly growing towns. New trade and craft schools, like the one established by the late Empress of Ethiopia in Addis Ababa, are springing up everywhere.

The attitude of the young Western-trained professional artist toward all this cannot be other than complex. As one teacher on a Ghanaian art faculty has put it: "in speaking of a contemporary art in Africa, distinction must be made between 'contemporary art in Africa,' 'contemporary African art,' and 'art in contemporary Africa.' " Thus in the galleries and museums of the African capitals, as well as in the homes and conversations of the intelligentsia, modern European painting and sculpture enjoys much the same prestige as in Paris or Milan. The abstract expressionist school of New York is well known in the art schools of Uganda and Ethiopia. Returning home from years of subsidized study in the schools and studios of Europe and America, the African artist feels impelled to teach Western theories and techniques. Hence, professional work in the galleries or student work in the art schools often seems very familiar to the visitor from the West.

Fortunately there is another side to the picture, for the pressure of African reality is very evident in the subject matter, if not the style, of most contemporary African painting and sculpture. In the new monumental architecture of government buildings, museums, and universities the demand is for an art that deals in intelligible terms with African experience. Naturally individual response to this demand varies widely. On my travels I met an impassioned young Ugandan painter who believed that the development of a national artistic idiom is a patriotic duty; and a very prosperous young Ethiopian artist whose work, which ranged from society portraits to stained glass for Coptic churches, would have found a ready market in Manchester or Kansas City. The issue is anything but resolved.

The posture of the young architect or city planner is much the same. In Europe and America he has seen in operation those technological processes which promise escape from the hunger, disease, and squalor that characterize the existence of so many of his countrymen. Very often the landscapes of his childhood, whether jungle village or urban slum, have become the hated symbol of life under colonial rule. Hence his receptiveness to our criteria of modern architecture and urbanism: for him, they have come to symbolize physical comfort, security, cleanliness, abundance. The unfortunate fact that American cities so seldom, or so unevenly, accomplish all this often escapes him. The glass-skinned skyscraper and shadeless street, the outward-looking house and open lawn, the wasteful automobile and sprawling suburb—all these are imported carte blanche.

The power of modern industrial technology is so great that, in purely formal terms, these African facsimiles can be quite

Tribal-dancing exhibition, Kenya

The "High Life," Accra, Ghana

Egyptian-born composer conducting street musicians, Addis Ababa, Ethiopia

Night-club band, Accra, Ghana

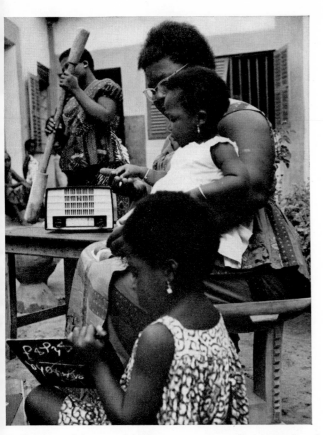

Radio entertaining grandchildren, servant pounding yams, Lomé, Togo

as well built as their Western prototypes. But, operationally, the results are often grotesque. Thus one sees cities of half a million where traffic jams are caused by the private cars of a minuscule elite and fantastically long queues wait for a few decrepit busses. Picture windows confront shadeless deserts. Air conditioners go mad in glass-walled skyscrapers in the Nigerian rain forests. Everywhere one sees heat-holding pavement instead of heat-deflecting foliage, open space where common sense dictates cover, transparency where opacity is the first requirement of comfort.

Despite many differences in history and culture, Egypt partially shares the artistic dilemma that faces the sub-Saharan states. This dilemma was dramatized for me by a visit made with an Egyptian friend, an architect and teacher in Cairo. We had gone together to the ancient Coptic enclave in the old quarter of the city. This extraordinary mud-walled remnant of the medieval city contains a magnificent museum of Coptic art: several Coptic churches (some of them dating from the sixth century); a Greek Orthodox church; a Jewish synagogue, centuries old; and cemeteries belonging to all three faiths. Around these extends a large residential quarter where poor people of these faiths, as well as some Moslems, live in harmony. By conventional criteria, the flies, dust, bad sanitation, and overcrowding make this a huge slum. But from another, and equally valid point of view, this is one of the best-designed districts of Cairo. The narrow streets, palm- and vine-shaded courtyards, thick mud walls, small windows, and inward-turning plans combine to make a sophisticated and urbane response to the merciless Egyptian climate.

Yet my young Egyptian friend, after a couple of hours, could stand it no longer. It was all very well, he told me, for foreigners to admire these picturesque medieval forms. But for a man who loved his country, who wanted to see it rebuilt on a more just and humane basis, this quarter, he said, was the stinking embodiment of everything he hated—ignorance, hunger, suffering, apathy. Normally a gentle man, he spoke with explosive wrath. For him it was literally not possible to breathe in such a milieu. I knew that his own grandparents, by God knows what combination of struggle and luck, had fought their way out of just such a situation, establishing the family on the edge of the modern middle-class world. He was too close to this quarter emotionally to view it with anything but blind repugnance.

Under such circumstances, it did little good to warn against throwing the baby out with the bath water. Nevertheless, it is precisely the task of his generation to avoid this mistake —to isolate the good from the bad, and the obsolete from what is still viable in his tradition. I heard the "open plan" and transparent wall of modern architecture praised by young intellectuals in this part of the world because, for them, it symbolized the liberation of the Moslem family from the crippling confinement of harem, purdah, and feudal relations generally. The fact that the desert sun, dust, and searing winds beat in through these newly opened walls did not disturb them. It was, they insisted, a small price to pay for the new social perspectives opened up.

But it must be perfectly clear to the outside observer that, in order for the new African architecture and urbanism to accomplish its minimum objectives, it must return to an attentive examination of its own pre-colonial origins. Two factors make this inevitable. On the one hand, even under the most favorable economic and technical conditions imaginable, it will be decades before Africa will have achieved the technological basis for Western architecture. And long before this is achieved, it will have become apparent that the Western prototype, whether in individual buildings or in whole cities, is ill-adapted to Saharan or equatorial Africa. The profoundly antipopular, antifunctional character of the new African cities is already sufficient proof of this.

Nationalism always carries the germ of zenophobia. But this danger, in the field of art and culture at least, does not seem to me very great in Africa today. Most young African intellectuals and artists have been trained in Western centers and have returned from this experience with a viewpoint of artistic and cultural possibilities that, if anything, is too cosmopolitan rather than too parochial. At the same time their new-found national consciousness and patriotism leads them to a growing interest in pre-colonial folklore of their own cultures. Under the circumstances of rapid industrialization, this new "artistic patriotism" seems to me to serve a useful function. At the very least, it interposes some barriers to the ruthless demolition of all preindustrial monuments and arts and crafts. At the best, it could result in an integration of primitive and postindustrial aesthetics to create new artistic idioms of unique value and world-wide significance.

The two tendencies—a fascination with the whole apparatus of Western technology and a growing understanding of the significance of their own past—create an ambivalent situation. The result is that Western and African modes of expression—in costume and cuisine, architecture and art, music and dance—coexist and compete. It would be hazardous indeed for an outsider to predict the outcome of this complex situation.

Only modern knowledge, modern science, modern technology, can give Africa the abundance and well-being it desires. But these forces can never be more than fertilizing agents and catalysts, acting on African resources, human and material. The Africans' greatest single resource for building their artistic and cultural future is their own indigenous past.

James Marston Fitch, professor of architecture at Columbia University, wrote about the preservation of Poland's architectural heritage in HORIZON *(Spring, 1964). Continuing his study of the uses of the past, he visited Africa last year.*

Selling yard goods, Niger

Ethiopian woman in traditional white shamma

MARC RIBOUD—MAGNUM

"Come as you are" in Ghana (left) and Kenya

Bold patterns, Lagos, Nigeria

Old-style mother, new-style child, Zaria, Nigeria

He is criticized for his jingoism, but Kipling is still read—and reread—
for his good yarns, his keen observations, and his bardic mastery of language

RUDYARD KIPLING: HE OUTLIVES THE EMPIRE

William Strang's etching of Kipling shows the author in the
midst of characters from his books. The elephant
and tiger at left, and Messua and her husband at lower left,
are taken from The Jungle Books. The ships' masts in
the background recall Captains Courageous; the crocodile
at lower right lived down by the great, gray-green,
greasy banks of the Limpopo River in the Just-So Stories.

By C. E. CARRINGTON

No one, I think, would dissent from the view that Kipling is one of those authors, like Mark Twain, like Dickens, like Dante—shall I dare to say?—who "date," whose work could not have been done quite as it was under any other circumstances. There are others, Virgil, for example, or William Blake, who might have made their highly personal contribution to literature with an equal effect if born in some other land or age, but Kipling was the expression of a phase of history. A portent in 1890, he had become an anachronism by 1930, and though we may be competent to criticize the 1890's, we are still too close to the 1930's to be sure of our ground. Kipling's reputation, therefore, now needs to be reappraised by a generation that rejects the fixed opinions not of its grandparents, who belonged to the age influenced by Kipling, but of its parents, who reacted against that influence. The fact that his name still has the power to evoke hatred, or love, or a combination of the two a generation after his death bears witness to his significance in social history.

For thirty or forty years Kipling was the world's bestselling author, in an age when the "fringe benefits" that authors now depend upon for a living did not exist. Between 1886, when his first published volume appeared in India, and his death in 1936 he produced about two hundred and fifty short stories, a thousand pages of ballads and lyrics, three or four longer works which may be described as novels, and some miscellaneous writings on history and travel. Almost the whole of this output has been repeatedly reprinted, and some few of his books remain obstinately in the class of "best sellers" even though the social and political opinions vulgarly associated with Kipling's name are altogether outmoded. His works have been translated into many languages, and some of them in recent years have even had a vogue in Soviet Russia. As the dictionaries of quotations reveal, he is among the half-dozen most frequently quoted English authors; and he is certainly the most misquoted. A fabulous monster bearing his name has been created, to the despair of those who read Kipling's work and protest in vain that he did not hold the views or express the opinions that are commonly ascribed to him.

In the world of politics such treatment of an opponent is —sad to say—frequent; the strange feature of the Kipling phenomenon is that reckless misstatement about the man and his work is to be found in the pages of the most sober and judicious literary critics, as when, in 1899, E. L. Godkin of the *Nation* wrote: "Kipling has long been to me a most pernicious vulgar person. . . . but I don't read him. I think most of the current jingoism on both sides of the water is due to him." "I don't read him" is the key phrase. Or again, when the English novelist H. E. Bates wrote in 1942: "No single syllable of Kipling's has ever given a moment's pleasure." Why this insistence? Why become so passionate about him? To take a recent instance, *The Pelican Guide to English Literature* has achieved a well-deserved success in Britain, but when the author comes to the 1890's, he abandons the

trade of criticism to present a figure of Kipling which has almost no historic resemblance to the original. He contents himself with selecting a few sentiments expressed by characters in Kipling's lesser juvenile pieces and assumes that the whole tone and content of the author's lifework can be derived from them. It is as if a writer on Shakespeare were to quote some outrageous remarks by Iago and Pistol as a sufficient account of the poetry and philosophy of the master.

So hostile is the approach to Kipling that his admirers are thrown on the defensive, and I shall therefore begin by protesting that the British Empire was the theme of only a small part of his work during only a short period of his life, and that much of what he wrote about the Empire was severely critical (most notably, perhaps, "The Widow at Windsor"). But why should it be necessary to clear away so many misconceptions before discussing what he actually wrote? Why should Kipling be condemned because he touched upon a theme that afterwards went out of fashion?

Kipling did not just appear: he exploded. A brash young man of twenty-four, he arrived in San Francisco in the fall of 1889, on his way to England from India, and laid a trail of indiscreet comments from the West Coast to the East. "Scores of men have told me with no false pride," he wrote in San Francisco, "that they would as soon concern themselves with the public affairs of the city or State as rake muck." "Now the mass of persons who vote is divided into two parties—Republican and Democrat. . . . the Democrat as a party drinks more than the Republican, and when drunk may be heard to talk about a thing called the Tariff . . ." "Most of the men wore frock-coats and top-hats . . . but they all spat." "There was wealth—unlimited wealth—in the streets, but not an accent that would not have been dear at fifty cents." At first he was not taken seriously, but when he became a celebrity, the American press began to react.

He reached London in October, unknown and poor, but endowed with a backlog of stories and ballads which had appeared in Indian newspapers during his seven years' hard labor as a journalist. He took the town by storm. Not only was he immensely prolific in 1890 with new work in verse and prose, but the reissue in England of his Indian ballads and stories provided a whole shelfful of best sellers in one season. Before his first London year was over he had published or republished eighty short stories, a volume of verse, the material for a second volume of verse, and a novel which aroused much discussion. The sensation was tremendous; from the beginning, this audacious young author was the subject of controversy, although it raged more violently in America than in England.

On his part, he started up a new conflict when he discovered, as other British authors had done before him, that there was then little or no protection for British literary property in the American copyright laws. His Indian stories were eagerly snapped up by American publishers who found the Kipling boom as profitable as did their British colleagues in London, and who could reprint these works without the formality of recompensing the author. It was when he discerned his error that Kipling first revealed those secretive and acquisitive traits of character that hardened as he grew older. Never again did he submit to casual interviews with newspapermen, and before the end of 1890 he engaged in a campaign against literary pirates which he maintained for the rest of his life. Since the battlefield was the United States, his love-hate relation with the American system then began to take shape.

Kipling's Indian output—*Departmental Ditties, Plain Tales from the Hills, Soldiers Three, Wee Willie Winkie*—is not the part of his work best known to modern readers. However, these were the stories and ballads that captivated London; for the first time they made the life of the British rulers in India intelligible to those who stayed at home. It was not the glamour of the Orient that he described but the tedium, the heat, and the disease that afflicted the empire builders as they struggled with social problems which they

. . ." he wrote. "But there is neither East nor West, Border, nor Breed, nor Birth,/When two strong men stand face to face." A week does not pass that the famous phrase is not used in a sense opposite to that which Kipling intended.

The theme which emerges is that in spite of the social snobberies of the capital (any capital), the crudity of army life (any army), and race prejudices (any race), only individuals count, and must be judged by their performance of their allotted task. Kipling's India has its heroes, but they are not the grandees of the Viceroy's court; they are the unnoticed or forgotten men who protect themselves by immersion in their daily routine—the bridge builders, the district officers, the subalterns, who respect above all their work and their colleagues. In the modern phrase, Kipling admired the "insiders." During his apprenticeship as a young journalist in India he had been one of them; in spite of discomfort and loneliness, he had known an inner happiness which he lost in London and did not quickly recover. Easy money, publicity, what the world calls success, as he soon found out,

Kipling ranks among the most popular targets of caricaturists—both friendly and unfriendly. At left, in a sketch by C. de Fornaro, Kipling is shown surrounded by some of the animals—including, in the upper right corner, one of the chattering Bandar-log—from The Jungle Books. *Max Beerbohm's caricature of Kipling as jingoist, at right, was captioned by Beerbohm, "Mr. Rudyard Kipling takes a bloomin' day aht, on the blasted 'eath, along with Britannia, 'is gurl."*

could not solve (and which are no nearer solution in these days of self-government). The best of the stories are cynical, detached, and knowing, as though the author spoke from the inside and could reveal a great deal more if he chose. *The Times* reviewer compared him with de Maupassant, and Oscar Wilde wrote that Kipling "had seen many remarkable things—through keyholes." The stories range over many aspects of Indian life, but the concentration of interest is on two groups of characters recurring in several stories—the idle and frivolous social circle of Mrs. Hauksbee, who pulled strings at Simla, the summer capital of India; and the listless, brutalized barracks life of British soldiers in the days when there was no refrigeration and no inoculation against tropical disease. The system was taken for granted, neither praised nor blamed, but as Kipling's technique developed and his knowledge of the world increased, he turned more and more to the topic of the dedicated men who served the system though it brought them neither profit nor credit. "Oh, East is East, and West is West, and never the twain shall meet

were no substitutes for being on the inside. In London, despite his success, he was an outsider.

Much of Kipling's early writing, reissued only to protect his copyright, was ephemeral stuff which has done his reputation some harm. What he wrote in London in 1890 and 1891 has far more depth, particularly the better wrought stories of soldiers in India (*The Courting of Dinah Shadd, Love-o'-Women, On Greenhow Hill*); and the tinkling light verse of *Departmental Ditties* was succeeded in 1892 by the richer harmonies of the *Barrack-Room Ballads*. (The later ballads are technically and emotionally stronger still.) But the climax of Kipling's literary life in London was the publication at the end of 1890 of *The Light that Failed*, his only true novel. Eagerly awaited and widely advertised, it had immense sales in serial and book form, both in Britain and America. It has been discussed and read from that day to this; it has been translated into many languages, dramatized at least once, and filmed three times. Yet it is a profoundly unsatisfying book, and the strangest part of its history is that it appeared almost simultaneously in two versions, one with a conventional denouement in which the hero marries the heroine, and one ending with the hero dying in Africa, rejected. What was not known when it was published was that the book was largely composed of actual episodes from the author's life, very slightly disguised, and recorded almost as they occurred. When the first draft was finished, in July, 1890, the author could hardly be sure whether his own love story was to have a happy ending. As he lived the romance he wrote it, using a plot borrowed from Mrs. Browning's *Aurora Leigh* as a framework into which he inserted episodes from his own experience. It is the book of an angry young man overflowing with spleen against a world whose favors he despised, but many a reader today, who picks it up and finds it distasteful, still cannot lay it down.

The first impression its author made on the public was that of a precocious, experienced young person who had been everywhere and tried everything, a sort of Dorian Gray. Some discerning critics of *The Light that Failed* observed that Kipling was not so knowing as he affected to be. His friend J. M. Barrie wrote, "His chief defect is ignorance of life. . . . He believes that because he has knocked about the world in shady company he has no more to learn"; while his venomous opponent Max Beerbohm wrote, with delicious mockery, "Strange that these heroes, with their self-conscious blurtings of oaths and slang, their cheap cynicism about the female sex . . . were not, as they so obviously seem to have been, fondly created out of the inner consciousness of a lady-novelist." All Kipling's graphic talents for giving verisimilitude by word painting could not evoke a deep meaning from the sequence of violent episodes in *The Light that Failed;* at heart it was a mawkish book, and the author could not make up his mind what he meant to say about sex. So far from being a man of wide experience, he had led a sheltered life in India in his parents' home. India had given him, so to speak, a studio in which to paint pictures rather than an arena in which to fight his own battle. It was in London, in the society described in *The Light that Failed,* that he first knew the rending passion of love, when a childhood sweetheart suddenly reappeared. He made her the Maisie of the novel. She was a painter, and the studio episodes in the book serve to remind us that Kipling had spent much of his young life in the company of painters. As in the book, so in real life the lady refused to abandon her art for marriage, and Kipling, in the autumn of his wander-year, was famous but wretched.

During those months he formed an association with a young American publisher, Wolcott Balestier, who, like Kipling, had made a sudden mark on London's literary life. It was Balestier who published the shortened version of *The Light that Failed* (the one with the happy ending), and it was probably Balestier who persuaded Kipling to make this concession to the novelettish market. For several months the two young men enjoyed a close friendship; after the copious production of the previous year, Kipling wrote little during this period besides his share of an indifferent romance, *The Naulahka,* which they issued in partnership. Then Kipling broke away to make a solitary voyage around the world, returning in haste when he received news that his friend had died of typhoid fever. Within ten days of reaching London he married Wolcott's sister, Caroline Balestier. This bald narration tells almost all that is known of the central event of Kipling's life, and this we learn chiefly from the letters of Henry James, a family friend of both the Kiplings and the Balestiers. It was James who described Rudyard as "the most complete man of genius . . . I have ever known."

*K*ipling's youth was now cut short. Essentially a domestic man, he was Carrie Balestier's husband for the remaining forty-five years of his life. She mothered him, she managed him, and she loved him, keeping the rest of the world at arm's length and protecting him from the intrusion of gossips, snobs, and journalists. She had golden fingers, and the money they made from his books multiplied. She kept a diary that recorded every house in which they slept, every friend who was admitted to their home. When children came, she established for him the "family square" on which he built his secure life. She provided the privacy and comfort in which he could work undisturbed, so that he began to write with deliberation, scrutinizing and revising every sentence. After his marriage, in 1892, the brash young journalist disappeared, to be replaced by a conscientious man of letters who was never shocking now unless he meant to be.

For four years they lived in Brattleboro, Vermont, where Mrs. Kipling owned a house, and some would say that this was the period of his best work (*The Jungle Books, Many Inventions, The Seven Seas, Captains Courageous, The Day's Work*). Life in New England, beginning as a happy honeymoon, gave him at first a deep satisfaction that was reflected in the mellower quality of his writing. The essence of Rudyard Kipling may be found in the two *Jungle Books* which are known to every literate nursery in the world. As he admitted, they were written on two levels, for children, and (especially in the "Mowgli" stories) for adults who were able to find a deeper meaning. The notion, borrowed from Emerson, of a man-child cast into the jungle and befriended by predatory beasts until, by accepting the law of the jungle, he learns to be its master, is a richer development of the lesson Kipling had learned in his unhappy early childhood. Sharing the common fate of British children in the days before the conquest of tropical disease, he had been sent away from his mother's care and placed under foster parents for a time. In India, too, he had experienced the loneliness of those human beings who can endure the harshness of the world only by concentrating on some immediate and useful task. But Mowgli, in the jungle, was exposed to a subtle temptation not unknown to young Kipling in London, the easy adulation of the monkey people, the Bandar-log, the chatterers in the treetops, who throw dirt at one another and who suppose that something has been achieved when it has been cleverly talked about. The London "monkey people" never forgave Kipling for his description of them.

Rudyard Kipling's range of interest was widely extended during his American period. He continued to produce reflective pieces about British India, both in verse and prose; he revealed a new talent in *The Jungle Books* for writing children's stories; and he introduced a new theme to literature, the romance of machinery. During the 1890's, while he roamed the English-speaking world, he had seen the engineer as a new type of man, a notion foreshadowed by Wordsworth and Whitman but left for Kipling to develop. He became the poet of the steam engine as Dickens was the novelist of the stagecoach; each of them thus fixed for us a passing phase of social history. In Kipling's world all depends on the man, the *artifex*; and the man can best retain his sanity in the new mechanical age by serving the machine faithfully until his expert knowledge allows him to become its master. As for the first-class passengers, the commuters who never know that "Romance brings up the nine-fifteen," they are of no more account than the Bandar-log. Kipling had an insatiable curiosity about mechanisms; he wanted to know what made things work, and to get beneath the skin of the man who did know, with the consequence that engineers and administrators—not great readers as a rule—read Kipling and quoted him to one another. In the phase into which the Western world was then passing, Kipling was the laureate of the worldmakers.

*B*ut before considering further this aspect of his work, I must dispose of the absurd family quarrel that sent Kipling scuttling home to England. As happy and prosperous as he was in Vermont, and as convenient as he found his working life there, he had difficulty in identifying himself with the life of the United States in the "gilded age"; and his American wife, now notably Anglicized, made the assimilation no easier for him. Their English accents and style of living were criticized in a conventional little town which considered them secretive and unneighborly. This failure to maintain good social relations became serious when a political crisis over Venezuela at the end of 1895 brought Britain and America to the verge of war. Kipling had sorrowfully made up his mind to align himself with his own country when a family feud hastened his departure. The quarrel between Rudyard Kipling and his ebullient brother-in-law, Beatty Balestier, each of them egged on by Kipling's wife, is possibly the most exciting thing that ever happened in Brattleboro. A long-smoldering dispute over family money, over Beatty's disreputable conduct, over remarks that the Kiplings were said to have passed among the neighbors, and finally over the ownership of the hay crop on a field which Beatty rented from Rudyard, ended in threats of violence—whereupon Rudyard very imprudently took his brother-in-

law into court. The gusts of publicity and ridicule which blew through the American press over this storm in a teacup gave Beatty all that he most enjoyed and Rudyard all that he most hated; and the considered comment on the episode must be that it curiously resembles one of those bitter, angry farces—*Brugglesmith, The Vortex, The Village that Voted the Earth was Flat*—which constitute a characteristic part of Kipling's work. A feature of his comic stories is the resolution of a tangle by the healing power of Gargantuan, openhearted laughter. But while the world laughed, he was unable to see the absurd side of his own village comedy. He fled from New England to Old England.

After a period of house hunting, the Kiplings settled in Sussex, and little remains to be said of their external lives except for their catastrophic return to America in 1899. They had business to attend to in New York and were cautiously considering a visit to Brattleboro when, in a very hard winter, the whole family became prostrated with feverish colds in an Eighth Avenue hotel. Rudyard and his elder daughter, Josephine (Taffy of the *Just-So Stories*), developed pneumonia, and for some days his life was despaired of. Then began a public demonstration of a kind unaccorded to any other man of letters. Kipling's reputation with the common people in many countries was so widespread that the progress of his illness made headlines in half the world. Traffic was stopped in Eighth Avenue by the crowds waiting in the snow for news, and people were seen kneeling in prayer at the hotel door. When it was announced that he had passed the crisis, that he was slowly gaining ground, the public manifestations were redoubled. Many days elapsed before the doctors dared to let the patient know that in the meantime his child Josephine had died, a personal tragedy that was of little interest to the public. It took him twelve months to recover from his illness, and he never recovered from the shock of his child's death; from that day a new tenderness, an added dimension, can be detected in his writing. Neither Rudyard nor Caroline was ever able to face the prospect of visiting America again.

After 1899 Kipling's doctors advised him to spend the winters in a mild climate. They decided on South Africa, where Cecil Rhodes offered them the use of a cottage on his estate near Cape Town. Kipling's youth had been spent in India and his young manhood in Vermont; his third home was in Africa. It was not until 1903 that he found a resting place in England, at the remote Sussex village of Burwash. His four hearths—in Asia, America, Africa, and Europe—had given him the freedom of the seas through which he had taken so many voyages; it is as the poet of *The Seven Seas* that we must now consider him.

This was the moment in history when the last secrets of the earth's surface were revealed, when the tropics and the arctic became accessible, when the railway, the steamship, and the telegraph cable for the first time brought all the continents and all the islands of the seas into direct contact. It was a Western triumph, the technological mastery of the world by the aggressive, inventive peoples of Europe and North America, the "White Men." What Kipling did was to reveal to his generation the nature of this unprecedented revolution in human affairs, and then to warn them against the moral dangers that world empire would arouse. His first endeavor in this field, after establishing his position as a tart critic of British India, was "The English Flag" (1891) with its memorable line, "And what should they know of England/ who only England know?" This was the first of a series of ballads presenting variations on a favorite theme: the activity of his countrymen, in all parts of the world, who accepted duty without conscious heroism, without reward, and without thanks. "If blood be the price of admiralty," he said, "Lord God, we ha' paid in full!" Or, more sentimentally, "Never the lotos closes, never the wild-fowl wake,/But a soul goes out on the East Wind that died for England's sake"; or, more cynically, "So some of us chivvy the slaver,/ And some of us cherish the black"; or, when his Calvinistic strain prompted him to a cosmic comment: "Predestination

congenial to the developer, the pioneer, and the engineer, while it reacted strongly against the crabbed obscurantism of the old Spanish Empire or of the Afrikaners (who were then very much what they are now).

Rudyard Kipling's comment on the two imperialist wars deserves closer examination. That it was desirable for the white man to develop South Africa he had no doubt, and that the British were better suited for the task than the Boers seemed to him no less evident. The Afrikaner system meant "laying on a new land evil of the old," but his ballads about the British Army in South Africa were fiercely critical, and he took the opportunity to scold the British public for its inadequacy while allowing some merit to the Boers for their simple virtues—as men. At the end of the war he was the first to call for reconciliation and a new union.

His great hymn of empire, a poem to which he gave the significant name "The Recessional," had been published shortly before the Boer War. So far from being a glorification, it was a solemn warning; so far from promising further

The Ruddikipple

This little Animal is very strong and vigorous and knows everything. If anybody tries to beat it, it brings out a fresh lott and then nobody cant touch that either. It stirs everybody up so it would make a peacepoo want to die for his country. If a foreign pounds his nose it just squashes him flat.

In 1898 Kipling was caricatured (at far left, from Punch *magazine's series "Animal Land") as a complacent toad. According to another contemporary cartoon, at left, Kipling drew inspiration for his poetry from such sources as "Cuss Rhymes and Slang" and "Bad Names." Not to be outdone by the professionals, Kipling once caricatured himself, at right, as a lazy, slightly stuffy, dunce.*

CARTOONS N.Y. PUB. LIB.

in the stride o' yon connectin'-rod." The message was always from and for the men overseas, the "White Men" dedicated to a task away from home, "where the new-raised tropic city sweats and roars," so that in the old countries homesickness was reversed by the impact of Kipling's phrasemaking, and stay-at-homes dreamed of far horizons "where the strange roads go down" and longed to be "somewheres east of Suez."

At the turn of the century England and the United States were involved in colonial wars which the present generation find it hard to understand, much less to justify—the Anglo-Boer War and the Spanish-American War. Though liberals in both Britain and America were disgusted and horrified at the time, and have since fixed their attitude of disapproval in the history books, the fact remains that men of moderate views and quiet tastes volunteered in the thousands to fight in South Africa or the Philippines, supposing themselves to be on the side of enlightenment. The spirit of the age, immensely stimulated by the geographical discoveries and mechanical devices that had made the world one place, was

growth, it foretold inevitable decline.

> *Far-called, our navies melt away;*
> *On dune and headland sinks the fire . . .*

And, in its plea against arrogance and for humility, it produced another of the gnomic sayings so often quoted in the opposite sense from that intended:

> *If, drunk with sight of power, we loose*
> *Wild tongues that have not Thee in awe,*
> *Such boastings as the Gentiles use,*
> *Or lesser breeds without the Law.*

The poem is a condemnation of imperial pride, and of those who boast when drunk with power. It is they, the unworthy empire builders, who are described as "lesser breeds," and the phrase cannot be construed as referring to the colonial peoples. He had a word for the Americans, too, in their imperial struggle. During the debates in the Senate over what should be done with the Philippine Islands he published his address to the American people, the poem "White Man's

Burden," which much impressed Theodore Roosevelt and Henry Cabot Lodge. It was an appeal to America to share in the task of developing the backward countries. This was a duty which would earn for those who undertook it "the blame of those ye better, the hate of those ye guard," while the reward—a typical Kipling note—would be nothing but "the judgment of your peers." Work and service are their own justification in his philosophy.

The man who had written so plainly that East and West *do* meet, in the direct confrontation of men with a sense of dedication, still had something to say about British India. In 1900 he at last completed a picaresque romance which he had rewritten several times. The reaction against imperialism was already setting in, so that Kipling's reputation with advanced thinkers was past its meridian, even though the sales of his books were steadily increasing. *Kim*, issued at an inauspicious moment, was coolly received and has been neglected by the critics. Surely it is the best book written by any European about India. It is infused with love for the land and the people, which distinguishes it sharply from E. M. Forster's spinsterish *A Passage to India*. Unlike Forster, Kipling has no political comment to make in *Kim*, although he has little that is favorable to say of the British ruling class. He is concerned with personal relationships in the underworld where castes and races mingle, and where the boy Kim, like Mowgli in the jungle, learns to accept the law of life. The same theme may be detected in *Stalky and Co.*, the rollicking school story written about the same time.

Lifting the lid off boy-life and revealing the crudities and barbarities that occur wherever boys are herded together was a process which revolted the stomachs of the sensitive, though boys liked the "Stalky" stories then and still enjoy them. Kipling never shirked the seamy side; he put into print a great many rough comments which would pass unnoticed in any smoking room but which were not thought decent in print fifty years ago. It is no defense to say that he was far surpassed in this respect by Hemingway and other admired writers of the post-Kipling era. There was in him a vindictive streak, which may be related to the Calvinistic tone of his philosophy. Retribution was inevitable and just in his scheme of things, and therefore to be observed with grim satisfaction—not a lovable quality but not uncommon.

With the publication of *Kim* he put Asia and all his impressions of the world East of Suez behind him. At thirty-five he still had half an active life before him. Rich and established, he lived in seclusion, visited only by his friends and by those whom he chose to admit to his circle, writing with deliberation, and publishing at longish intervals new volumes of prose stories interspersed with verses. One episode broke the even tenor of his routine—the death of his only son in the First World War. His two bereavements—the daughter who died in America and the son who died in Flanders—left gaps that were never closed, and exposed new depths in his personality.

For some years he turned his penetrating eye back upon English history and wrote of it with the same wealth of revealing detail that had made his phrases about the Seven Seas memorable. Technically the "Puck" stories are among his most accomplished, and the verses that go with them come nearest to that pure poetry which he rarely achieved. Kipling never spoke of himself as a poet. As he grew older and more mature (the public and private calamity of the war had had its effect), a strain of pessimism that had never been lacking in his nature became more evident. This later Kipling, to whom the serious critics have at last begun to give attention, shared a philosophy with Thomas Hardy and showed literary resemblances to Henry James, two older men who were among his friends.

Writing, as he then did, upon themes and about characters which seemed to belong to a different society from that of the soldiers and empire builders of his youth, Kipling still infused every sentence he wrote with a grave intensity. He was still the same man and, probing deeper into the hearts of his characters, he still found the old qualities. The loneliness of Mowgli and Kim, and their necessity to adjust to an alarming world, remained the predicament of the indomitable old ladies, surgeons, and civilians in wartime whom he put under the microscope in his later stories. A recurrent theme is the "breaking-strain," the intolerable burden of the twentieth century which demands of simple human beings more than they can bear. This was his commentary on the First World War, expressed in verse epigrams with a Horatian neatness and force, and in several stories, written with a rich contexture of motives and themes, that were utterly unlike the externally observed stories of his Indian days.

The volume *Debits and Credits*, published in 1926 when he was sixty years old, contains six stories which would establish Kipling as one of the world's greatest storytellers if he had published nothing else. The enlarged range, the wide variety of topics, the deeper insight, and the fully mastered technique of these later stories yet reveal, in every sentence, the personality of the man who had given such a stimulus to the English-speaking peoples in 1890. His political opinions he knew to be outmoded; his ethical principles were unaltered. The "Gods of the Copy-book headings," he wrote, would resume their sway. But it is significant that his later stories have more heroines than heroes, that the memorable characters are middle-aged women (like Helen Turrell in *The Gardener* and Mrs. Ashcroft in *The Wish House*) whose abiding love knows no breaking-strain. This seems to have been his last reflection on an age which he disapproved of, and on a society which he saw to be heading for disaster. He died in 1936 before it came.

C. E. Carrington has written several books on the British Empire—notably The British Overseas—*as well as the authorized biography of Kipling,* The Life of Rudyard Kipling.

KIPLING'S INDIA

PHOTOGRAPHS BY BRIAN BRAKE—MAGNUM

Kipling's India was British India, "the brightest jewel" in the Empire's diadem. It was a country of splendid Hindu temples, the Taj Mahal, maharajahs, and silver howdahs, of the sacred white cow, the sacred Ganges, and street bazaars—all watched over by the British Viceroy, an efficient civil service, and a few regiments of fighting Englishmen. The British had their clubs, and gentlemen played cricket. In 1902, when Edward VII succeeded Victoria to the throne, the coronation durbar in Delhi outshone even the celebration in London.

Since 1947, the year of India's independence, that sprawling, crowded subcontinent has changed a great deal. Yet much of Kipling's India remains. The native soldiers are still divided into the regiments organized by the British; their officers affect swagger sticks and carry themselves with a Sandhurst bearing. When the Indians celebrate their Republic Day, with parades such as the one above in New Delhi, they march through the Central Vista along Processional Way, toward the All-India War Memorial. The Vista, the Way, the Memorial— indeed, all of New Delhi—was planned by Sir Hugh Keeling, Sir Alexander Rouse, Sir Edwin Lutyens, and Sir Herbert Baker. In India's Supreme Court, and in Parliament, the language is English. Tommy Atkins is gone, of course, and Gunga Din now seems remote, but it will be many years before British India, as Kipling knew it, disappears altogether. Its impact has been too pervasive. Gentlemen today—Indian gentlemen—play cricket, and Jawaharlal Nehru was ushered into the next world to the accompaniment of the old English hymn, "Abide With Me."

The mood and manner
of an earlier era

Unchanged from colonial days, the Gymkhana Club is now an exclusive gathering place for officials of the Indian government—as it was, originally, for members of the British civil service. The club was formed from the old Lawrence and Montgomery halls. Sir John Lawrence, British Viceroy in the Punjab from 1864–69, helped to organize a civil service in his province that became a model for the British. It was his branch of the service—paternalist, dedicated to public works—that so captivated Kipling's imagination and, through Kipling's writings, came to typify Britain's administration of India. As the Indians have perpetuated the British clubs and the old privileges of the service so, too, have they perpetuated much of Britain's military pageantry. At the final twilight ceremony of Republic Day the mounted guard at the Secretariat and the blue-jacketed Jaipur 61st Cavalry recall an earlier era of pomp and circumstance.

THE GYMKHANA CLUB, LAHORE

GUARDS AT THE SECRETARIAT BUILDING, REPUBLIC DAY

THE JAIPUR 61ST CAVALRY, REPUBLIC DAY

THE GOLDEN TEMPLE, AMRITSAR

BRASS BAZAAR IN THE PUNJAB

Side by side:

ancient India,

unchanged by

British colonials . . .

. . . and the stamp

of colonial Britain,

unchanged by

independent India

Amritsar, the religious capital of the Sikhs, has been traditionally a site for bloody skirmishes—among the Sikhs themselves. Its temple, at upper left, was built in the sixteenth century, destroyed in *1761,* rebuilt in *1764,* and finally, in *1802,* gilded with copper (to acquire its present name, the Golden Temple) by Ranjit Singh. "We of the Loodhiana Sikhs," a Sikh soldier said to Kipling's hero Kim, "do not trouble our heads with doctrine. We fight." Encountered, but left unchanged, by the British, Kipling's Sikhs proudly maintain their ancient customs: the neighborhood around the Temple is prime recruiting territory for today's Indian army. The bazaars Kipling spoke of remain, too, much as they were before the British arrived in India. The brass bazaar at left recalls Kipling's description, in Kim, of the Lahore bazaars, "hot and crowded" places where a man confronts "the press of all the races in Upper India."

Born in Bombay, in the typical colonial home seen opposite above, Kipling lived there until he was six years old. After ten years of schooling in Britain, Kipling returned to that vast city again. In his dedication for The Seven Seas Kipling wrote, "Comfort it is to say:/ Of no mean city am I." Yet it was Lahore, and *not* Bombay, that Kipling knew best. He was a member of the Punjab Club (opposite below, since converted to an Administrative Staff College for Indian civil servants), where, as he once said, ". . . bachelors, for the most part, gathered to eat meals of no merit among men whose merits they knew well." In Lahore Kipling worked for a newspaper and developed into a professional writer; and it was India that he remembered as his first love: ". . . no man breaks wholly loose/ From his first love, no matter who she be. . . ./ We've only one virginity to lose,/ And where we lost it there our hearts will be!"

KIPLING'S BIRTHPLACE, BOMBAY

THE FORMER PUNJAB CLUB, LAHORE

Good-bye, Puffing Billy
Good-bye, flower beds
Good-bye, rural England
Hello, traffic jam

One day back in 1935 the management of Britain's Southern Railway (as it then was) announced its intention to close the narrow-gauge branch line from Lynton to Barnstaple in North Devon. The proposal was received by the local inhabitants with angry consternation. For them, the tall-chimneyed locomotives, the little flower-bordered stations, and the slender thread of two-foot-gauge rails coiling along the steep contours of the Devon combes had become as much of an institution as village church or pub. Moreover the line ran through the heart of a popular tourist district. What would the holiday maker do without it? Closure had seemed unthinkable, yet now some busybody official in remote London was threatening to destroy it with a stroke of the pen.

Mounting local indignation culminated in a protest meeting at Barnstaple, where the crowd was joined by a strong and very vocal contingent from the other end of the line at Lynton. The meeting seemed to be going well for the railway supporters until the chairman politely inquired how many of the Lynton deputation had traveled to Barnstaple by train. Out of the embarrassed silence that followed there emerged the horrid truth that, to a man, the Lynton champions had come by highway. The fate of the Lynton & Barnstaple was sealed.

This sad little story was prophetic of the shape of things to come. It is also typical of the curiously ambivalent attitude of many an Englishman toward his railways. Dissatisfied with the age of sheet metal, plastics, and reinforced concrete in which he finds himself, the Englishman regards wistfully and with growing affection the more substantial, enduring, self-confident, and individualistic products of the Victorian era. Of that age Britain's railways are the most eloquent and omnipresent reminder. The soaring spans of a viaduct, bestriding some remote valley with so sublime an assurance of permanence; the classic proportions of a blackened-stone tunnel portal; the fanciful "cast-iron Gothic"

Old-fashioned railroading, with well-kept steam power and all-separate-compartment carriages, lingers on the Isle of Wight. Opposite is a local from Ryde Pier Head to Newport.

OLIVER JENSEN

Flowers brighten a station on the Isle of Wight, whose remaining railways are scheduled to close this October—despite bitter local opposition and their attractions for tourists.

tracery supporting a glass platform canopy, or the crow-stepped brick gables of some sleepy country station in East Anglia; the elaborate paneling of an early six-wheeled passenger coach or the elegant brass-beaded curves of the driving-wheel splashers of a steam locomotive—such Stephensonian splendors, once ridiculed or ignored, are now fast becoming as highly prized and as carefully studied as the architectural intricacies of our medieval churches. But just as the Englishman would resolutely defend his village church against any despoiler yet seldom if ever kneels in its pews, so he seldom patronizes his village railway station. Rather than do so he will endure the barbaric rigors of modern road transport, resignedly taking his place in an interminable stop-and-go line of commuter traffic or standing in pouring rain at a curbside to wait for an already overcrowded bus. Yet if this same road traveler, patient under every assault on his nerves and health, turns to the rails, he will at once complain that there was no fire in the

GEORGE PERRY

station waiting room, that his carriage was dirty, that his train was ten minutes late, and that the whole railway system had become an anachronism.

Ever since Britain's railways were nationalized shortly after the last war, their annual deficit has mounted until by 1962 it reached a painful figure. With intent to check this financial rake's progress, the British government secured from Imperial Chemical Industries, Ltd., the services of Dr. Richard Beeching, one of its top executives, and placed him at the head of the British Railways Board with a mandate to make the railways pay. Seldom has any executive held a hotter seat, and to give him his due, Dr. Beeching has so far succeeded in keeping remarkably cool, considering the hot blasts of controversy that daily beat into

EDGAR T. MEAD, JR.

A living reproach to the Beeching theories is the financial health of the Talyllyn Railway, a private narrow-gauge line in Wales whose carefully restored old cars are well patronized. This train is pulled by the ancient Edward Thomas.

his office in what was once the Great Central Railway Hotel at Marylebone Station, London.

As soon as he was appointed, Dr. Beeching initiated what is certainly the most detailed and protracted statistical survey of Britain's railway system that has ever been carried out. The results of this survey and the proposals based on them were published in 1963. This "Beeching Report," as it is popularly called, advocated the closure of no less than 2,363 stations and halts and 266 lines, mostly in rural areas, totaling 5,000 route miles. Only by such drastic pruning, Beeching claims, can the railways hope to recover financial health, but on the future profitability of the lopped-off remainder which is to survive his axe, the Doctor is distinctly guarded in his forecasts.

The Beeching Report has provoked on a national scale precisely the same storm of controversy that raged locally at Barnstaple nearly thirty years ago. So far its author has ridden this storm with great skill and subtlety. The weakness in the opposition's case is that same curious inconsistency in the Englishman's attitude to railways that lost the day at Barnstaple, and in his published statements Dr. Beeching has cleverly exploited it by presenting the issue as a choice between muddleheaded sentiment on the one hand and the cool, clear light of economic truth on the other.

By such tactics he doubtless hopes to discredit those who question whether his economics do in fact present so clear a light of truth as he would have us believe, and who quote the old saying about figures lying and liars figuring. We are all too apt, in this day and age, to regard figures with reverential awe, as if they were revelations of absolute truth—it is perhaps time we realized that accountancy is an art and not an exact science. An expert accountant can use his figures as an artist does his colors to produce the desired effects of light and shade. The most brilliant colorist would not claim to be able to capture on canvas more than a pale shadow of reality, and to pursue this analogy, Dr. Beeching's statisticians used a very limited palette indeed.

Through the whole length of Britain, from Lands End to John o' Groat's, Beeching's men zealously set about their task, calculating the revenue per train mile on the Highland line from Dingwall to the Kyle of Lochalsh or totting up the booking-office receipts at Bishop's Nymptom and Molland in deepest Devonshire. They ignored the conditions prevailing on the most overcrowded and inadequate highway system in the world, where belated and costly roadworks prove powerless to free a mounting congestion that represents an incalculable financial loss in wasted time, energy, and fuel. To anyone familiar with this chaos the solemn pronouncements of Dr. Beeching's experts read like something out of *Alice in Wonderland*. Each summer, queues of frustrated holiday-bound motorists grow miles long on the narrow roads to East Anglia, to the West Country, to Wales, and to Scotland, yet Beeching tells us that the railways in these areas must close. Ask why and the answer comes pat: because holiday railway traffic represents an inadequate utilization of motive power and rolling stock and so cannot be justified economically.

The experts apply precisely the same argument to urban commuter traffic. It is not economical, they tell us, to provide reserves of power and rolling stock for use only during the brief morning and evening rush-hour periods. Consequently many commuter services and suburban stations are also threatened by the Beeching axe. The unfortunate commuter has been told that the only economic alternative to the withdrawal of services is a fare increase so steep that it would undoubtedly defeat its own object. The commuter would take to the road rather than pay so dearly for the privilege of clinging, half-suffocated, to a strap in an overcrowded train.

Despite the frantic demolition of ancient buildings and pretty villages to make way for the new belt highways, overpasses, and traffic circles which are so speedily converting the environs of Britain's historic cities and towns into featureless deserts of concrete and macadam, urban traffic chaos worsens perceptibly each month as more mass-produced cars pour onto the roads. We speak patronizingly of the "Railway Mania" that seized the staid Victorians in the 1840's, but it was a mild aberration compared with the Motor Mania that bedevils us today. In these circumstances it is clear that if Dr. Beeching implements his plan, either by closure or fare increase, he will the sooner bring urban road traffic to that final grinding halt toward which it is surely heading. To get it moving again, if that is possible at all, the government will be forced to spend on disfiguring highways and car-parks many times over what it saves on railways. Governments, of course, spend their money from different pockets, and it is only the taxpayer who spends from just one.

One economist (unmentionably heretical according to the canons of Beeching and his school) has argued that it would pay Britain handsomely if railway travel were made free. This argument is by no means so fanciful as it may appear at first thought: if the criterion of high utilization upon which the Beeching plan has been based were to be applied to the automobile, some highly interesting facts would emerge. Consider, for example, the case of the daily car commuter who travels, say, ten miles to work. It may take him an hour to cover this distance—and for a high proportion of this time he will be simply standing still, with engine running, alone in a vehicle designed to carry at least four people. Having reached his place of work, the commuter may waste further time and fuel in the frustrating search for a vacant parking space before he leaves his car standing idle for the day. Dr. Beeching's economists would unhesitatingly condemn this whole operation as preposterously wasteful and unprofitable.

From this viewpoint the worthy Doctor's cool, clear light of economic truth begins to look a little dim, and his jocular dismissal of his antagonists as so many sentimentalists dreaming nostalgically of the good old days seems more than a little specious. Beeching has been regarded by too many people as the personification of mid-twentieth-century commercial expertise, a kind of secular high priest whose doctrines are infallible, whereas in truth his prescription for railway health is compounded of economic dogmas older than the railways themselves. The railways are not only the victims of sentiment but also of the curious prevailing view that because a thing is old it must necessarily be inefficient and out-of-date. Indeed, the sentimental and the so-called "realistic" views are closely allied and help to explain the Englishman's ambivalent attitude with which Beeching has made such play. Yet, whereas the railways, intelligently used, could play a great part in solving the overwhelming transportation problem that confronts a grossly overcrowded urban society, the one-sided application of nineteenth-century economics can only bring complete chaos the nearer. In other words it is not the railways that have become anachronistic but Dr.

Beeching's medicine, which carefully cures a limb while allowing the rest of the body to bleed to death.

Tourists, commuters, and the inhabitants of the more remote parts of Britain will be the first victims of the Beeching plan, but their plight will be only one consequence of the pursuit of the high utilization obsession. At British collieries it has always been the practice to store coal in railway wagons on a fan of sidings at the pit head to avoid double handling. Until 1947 such wagons were the property of the colliery company, but when the mines and railways were nationalized, the "private-owner-wagon" system was abolished and all rolling stock became the property of British Railways. Now, the prospect of idle wagons standing at the pit head is anathema to Dr. Beeching's experts, who insist that all

EDGAR T. MEAD, JR.

Safe from Beeching's grasp on the semi-autonomous Isle of Man is this splendid private 3-foot-gauge steam railway. Above is a scene on the Douglas-Port Erin line. Man also has wooden trolleys, horsecars, and a mountain cog-railway.

wagons must be kept rolling. Indeed, their economic ideal is a kind of demented *perpetuum mobile*. Hence the collieries must either provide new coal-storage facilities or the National Coal Board must pay British Railways a ransom in wagon demurrage. This, of course, means a head-on collision between two huge and tottering nationalized giants and, as usual, the British public will be the only loser whichever way the battle goes. The most likely outcome is that Alfred Robens, the National Coal Board boss, will cock a snook at Beeching by investing in new and larger fleets of road vehicles, forsaking Britain's railways as he has already forsaken her canals and thus making a further handsome contribution to ultimate highway chaos.

Again, it was the same high utilization obsession that led British Railways, before the Beeching era, to abandon its newly designed range of steam locomotives in favor of diesels costing from two to three times as much per unit. British

Railways is still groaning under the financial burden of this switchover. In a country with no native oil resources this motive-power policy was justifiable solely on the grounds of the higher utilization of the diesel as compared with steam. Experience in America, it was argued, had proved that a diesel could run 300,000 miles a year, a utilization figure that no steam locomotive could approach. Such a figure more than offset the high capital cost because far fewer diesel locomotives would be required to run Britain's railways.

Unfortunately there are fatal flaws in this argument. The figure of 300,000 miles per annum was achieved in selected transcontinental express service. In general service in the United States the locomotive utilization figure falls to an average of 80,000 miles a year, while under railway operating conditions in the island of Britain, general-service mileage figures could not approach this. These facts shed a very different light on the picture, especially when experience outside Britain has shown that the economic life of the diesel is only twelve to fifteen years as compared with thirty-five to forty for steam. Meanwhile steam locomotives of classic design, little Puffing Billies and big ones alike, with many years of useful life left in them, are being butchered wholesale.

It would seem logical to develop and improve railway communications in districts where roads inadequate for modern traffic could be widened and straightened only at vast and unwarrantable cost. Such are the narrow, high-banked, switchback roads of England's West Country and those that thread the mountains of central Wales and the Highlands of Scotland. Improved transportation facilities in these areas are essential unless holiday motorists are to be banned from visiting them and if—far more important—the local populations are to be prevented from ebbing away to already overswollen cities. Rail services in these areas have deteriorated till they have become virtually unusuable except by the most determined railway enthusiast, and now they are about to be finished off. Conversely, millions have been poured without stint into the task of electrifying the old main line of the London & North Western Railway from Euston through Crewe to Manchester and Liverpool. This route is not only menaced by the competition of intercity air services but it is closely paralleled throughout by new motorways. Never mind; our railway experts are convinced that their new electrified line can win back traffic from both. The public, of course, knows very little of technicalities and costs; it has been led to believe that the growing deficit is due solely to loss of traffic to the roads and that the Beeching Plan is unpalatable but essential. However, those of us who have seen the millions of dollars being poured into projects that are, to say the least, technically and commercially questionable, see Beeching as a man preparing to chop up the staircase for fuel to keep the fire alight because his gambling debts do not enable him to pay his coal bill.

Some lines, alas, have already suffered under the axe. Not many months ago British Railways published a beautiful color poster exhorting tourists to travel by rail to see the beauties of Breconshire. Hardly had this appeared on the hoardings before every railway line into the county was closed down, leaving the town of Brecon remote from any rail communication. There was a time when no fewer than four railway companies considered it worthwhile to serve this lovely shire and its capital. The most spectacular of these was the Brecon & Merthyr.

Leaving Brecon, the Merthyr-bound train clattered easily along beside the waters of the Usk until it drew to a halt at the little riverside station of Talybont-on-Usk. It then headed due south, tackling the formidable barrier of the Brecon Beacons, which divides the Usk Valley from South Wales, by one of the most dramatic railway routes in Britain. The seven miles of 1-in-38 grade from tree-shaded Talybont to the moorland summit tunnel at Torpantau, 1,300 feet above sea level, was so exacting a test of motive power that, years ago, the engineer Robert Fairlie used it as a testing ground for his articulated locomotives which for so long hauled the trains of the Mexican railways over the Orizaba mountains. In its laboring ascent the little train clung to the steep mountain slopes like a Welsh sheep and looked no larger in the scale of that landscape. But now those mountain walls echo its laboring exhaust-beats no longer, and it is unlikely that the narrow, vertiginous mountain road that parallels its route will ever carry that "alternative bus service" always so glibly but delusively promised when a train service is withdrawn. Breconshire soon felt the weight of its loss when the snow blocks of an arctic winter brought all road traffic in the shire to a standstill.

Enterprising management would long ago have exploited the beauties of these lines which bring the scenic splendors of Wales closer to the tourist than do any of Breconshire's inadequate roads. No such effort was made. It has been left to amateur railway enthusiasts, running two little narrow-gauge lines in North Wales, the Talyllyn and the Ffestiniog railways, to show what could be done in this way. On the Talyllyn, tourist traffic has been increased more than fivefold in ten years—but, there now, we know that Dr. Beeching is not interested in holiday traffic. The experts assure him that it is uneconomical, and experts cannot be wrong.

The immediate surroundings of the modern motor road or airport look very much alike whether one is in Old England or New England. These manifestations of the machine age numb the human spirit into insensibility, and ignore two golden rules: that man cannot live by bread—or mere utility—alone, and that variety is the spice of life. Railways are the last great machine-age development to possess that variety.

Until recently, the railway stations of Britain, also infinite in their variety, had remained almost unscathed. There was nothing quite like the British country railway station anywhere else in the world. The nineteenth-century railway architects designed them in every style but with a common purpose—to assure a conservative and apprehensive rural population that the new steam monster was really highly respectable. Hence the squire's stone-built lodge with its classical portico, or the cottage *orné* with its crow-stepped Flemish gables of stone-faced brickwork, became the prototype for station buildings. Hence, too, the bright flower beds on the station platforms. It was just because it was deliberately designed to make the countryman feel at home that the country station slipped so graciously into the country scene.

"A poor life this if, full of care,/ We have no time to stand and stare." Standing (or sitting) and staring, contemplating the follies of the mysterious world into which we are willy-nilly thrust, is an occupation essential to our spiritual well-being, and there is no better place to do it than the platform of a country station on a summer's afternoon. The occasional rumble of rich dialect voices from porter's room or signal cabin matches the murmur of bees among the flowers. And one seems far removed from the strain of modern life. Yet occasional intervals of well-ordered but unhurried activity— the ping of the telegraph bell, the clunk of a pulled signal lever and the whisper of its wire, the smooth passage of the predestined train—somehow make the station a more effective medicine than the complete solitude of the desert island we sometimes crave. Moreover, in an hour thus spent, or in the corner seat of a stopping, or local, train calling at many such stations, one can learn more about Britain than one could in a thousand miles of motoring. We thought the village railway station as inviolable as the village pub, but we were wrong.

When the railway pioneers brought the first great trunk line into London, Thomas Hardwick celebrated their triumph over almost impossible odds by designing for the entrance of the new Euston station a gigantic Doric portico of stone. It was the finest flower of railway-station architecture, and its demolition by British Railways in the face of great opposition was one of the worst acts of architectural vandalism ever perpetrated in any capital city. Yet its fall was aptly symbolic of what was to come, for its destruction has since been re-enacted on a smaller scale all over the country, and the process is still going on not only on the branch lines but on the main lines as well. The diesel-hauled expresses carrying bored businessmen from city to city roar past dozens of ruined station buildings and torn-up platforms. It is as though, when Hardwick's mighty columns fell, all else fell with them to ruin, defeatism, and despair.

Posters still exhort visitors and vacationers to "SEE BRIT-AIN BY TRAIN," but the slogan is fast becoming an empty one. Who, for the pleasure of it, would choose merely to join the businessmen on their fretful intercity journeys?

The British Travel & Holidays Association, which spends large sums of government money annually in cajoling dollar tourists to "Come to Britain," will have their work cut out in the future in trying to persuade Americans to join the fume-laden, bumper-to-bumper traffic jams on the British highways, for of this the Americans get a-plenty at home.

The final, decisive battle for Britain's railways is likely to be fought in the Highlands of Scotland. Much thought and money have been devoted in an attempt to check the depopulation of the Highlands by subsidizing the crofters, by bringing new industries to the glens and the islands, and by developing the tourist trade. In this great area of mountain and moor, motor roads are necessarily few and inadequate and often snow-blocked in winter. Railways are the essential lifelines. In the strictly comparable highlands of Norway the Norwegian government subsidizes railways because it recognizes that they are an essential service. The annual deficit on the working of the Scottish Highland lines is substantially less than that of the Norwegian State Railways, yet they are to be lopped off. And if this happens, there will be no railways

PAUL HOCQUARD

England is not yet the auto-dedicated country America is. When little Settle, Yorkshire (pop. 2,455), loses this pretty station, the natives will be hard put to arrange their travels.

north of Inverness, no iron roads to the Isles, to Oban or the Kyle, or to Wick and Thurso in the farthest north.

The clansmen are sharpening their claymores and preparing to sweep over the border as they did in 1745 to take Dr. Beeching's Marylebone stronghold by storm. Will they succeed? And if they do so, will not the Celts of Wales and the West Country and the Saxons of East Anglia rise and rally to their cause? As the Highland train sweeps round the magnificent curving viaduct of Glenfinnan, the passenger looks down upon the spot where Prince Charles Edward once raised his standard. Perhaps another standard will be defiantly planted there soon, and with better fortune.

L .T. C. Rolt, a mechanical engineer educated at Cheltenham College, is a railway buff, an old-car fancier, and a leading writer on the Industrial Revolution. He has been closely associated with the revival of the Talyllyn Railway in Wales.

ALL PHOTOGRAPHS BY THE AUTHOR EXCEPT WHERE OTHERWISE NOTED

IN PRAISE OF STAIRS

An Elegy by BERNARD RUDOFSKY

To speak of the ups and downs of stairs would sound like punning, had history not left a graphic record of their shifting importance. In the past, stairs always ranked with the noblest elements of architecture. Ascending or descending a flight of stairs called for a display of grace unmarred by any outward signs of physical exertion, while steps leading to altars and thrones imposed a veritable ritual of movement. Architects were obsessed with building monumental, not to say transcendental stairs, seeing in them a symbol of man's desire to rise above the commonplace. The fabled ziggurats and hanging gardens of old were truly apogees of stairs. So would be the Tower of Babel if that ambitious project had not been thwarted by the Lord.

Ever since man failed to get to heaven by way of stairs, their importance has declined, reaching its lowest ebb in our day. At a time when only underprivileged people walk, when the word "pedestrian" has become synonymous with dull and slow, stairs barely survive as back stairs. Flatfooted, down-to-asphalt industrial man is loath to assault as much as a single flight of them. He considers climbing stairs as atavistic as climbing trees. Besides, stairs have been largely superseded by machines: escalators, elevators, chair lifts, and cable cars. Except in domestic architecture, stairs are but a last resort, to be used only when other means of vertical transportation fail.

America's contribution to the world of stairs is fire escapes—architectural hardware of identical runs and landings never intended to be climbed; to be descended, fittingly, only when life is in danger. Born of greed rather than poverty, they have no beauty: entrails of houses shamelessly flung over walls and windows alike.

Stairs have of course other uses than just a climb. To this day the amphitheatres of antiquity and the vast stairscapes of the Old World are ideal gathering places. In climates less dour than ours, outdoor stairs extend a constant invitation to sit down. Such stairs are not merely accessories to buildings but a sort of germinating ingredient—the leaven in the architectural dough, so to speak. Yet whatever their finer points, stairs are only as good as their climbers. If we ever learn to walk again, they may once more find their rightful place in our lives.

The main street of a hill town in southern Italy

The Monumental

Rome, the grandest of Italian hill towns, has an abundance of stairs unequaled anywhere in the world. A complicated topography, and a populace with an insatiable appetite for pomp, spurred architects to devise panoramic staircases for social and mercantile activities. The Piranesi engraving above portrays the busy Ripetta, the old harbor on the Tiber, built at the beginning of the eighteenth century to the plans of Alessandro Specchi. Unfortunately, the stagelike setting has long since been sacrificed to regulation of the river.

The Scala di Spagna (left) is far more than a stairway in the accepted sense of the word. It is a civic forum, a *salone*, a promenade, and only incidentally a passage from the Piazza di Spagna to the church of SS. Trinità dei Monti. It is so ingeniously designed that few people ever notice its asymmetry. The runs and landings—two rather inappropriate terms for these cascades of steps—are worlds apart from our escalators intended to transport inert humans like so many parcels on a conveyor belt.

Like many another Roman landmark, the Piazza del Campidoglio is a walk-up. Access to this fine Renaissance square and its buildings is provided by five staircases, some climbing from the street level and some descending from neighboring heights. The flight of steps opposite, leading out of the south corner of the square (to Monte Caprino), is remarkable for its aggressive clarity.

The Vernacular

Some of the finest stairscapes have been composed without benefit of drafting boards. The Old World is chock-full of superb free-wheeling stairs, unmentioned and unnoticed by art historians. The precarious mountain paths cut into live rock, the irregular steps winding their way through steep hill towns, the heavenly ladders ascending to pilgrimage churches in Latin countries, or to temple sites on holy mountains in China and Japan—all these are anathema to addicts of drive-in architecture. Those of us, however, who are still in command of our legs, and who like to temper exercise with reverie, find the settings of these informal stairs bristling with mythological and classical associations.

Goat-footed climbers disdainful of bannisters and landings may want to scale the sirens' islands, Li Galli (left, above), in the Gulf of Salerno, once a landmark on the route of Ulysses, now the summer residence of the famous choreographer Leonide Massine. The stepped ramps (left, below) that lead from the harbor of the Greek island Thera, also known as Santorin, to its capital Phirà, may appeal only to those with the endurance of a mule, for the difference in elevation is 660 feet, the equivalent of sixty-six floors. And the view from the top is not for timid souls: a circular wall of precipitous rocks encloses a water-filled crater, from whose midst rise the vapors of an active volcano. For lazybones, there are the labyrinthine stairways of Sperlonga (opposite). The town strikes one as being one huge building with narrow passageways and steep flights of steps, cool and fragrant with the exhalations of a Mediterranean fishing village.

FRENCH TOURIST OFFICE

The Rhetorical

Among the offshoots of baroque architecture are what might be called operatic staircases—scenographic compositions of flights to serve as foils for social functions. Quite logically, such stairs are not tucked away in the corners of buildings; they boldly assert their presence. The grand staircase (above) at the Opéra in Paris was built by Charles Garnier in the 1860's. Animated by a first-night audience, the marble mountain of acclivities and lookouts with vistas of the wealthy and famous presents enchanting trails for social climbers. When architects had wasp waists rather than urban renewal on their minds, they dreamed up curvy stairs like those in the department store Dufayel in Paris (right). Even the torrents of ornamental detail do not detract from the daring contours. A painter's tribute to the fascination of stairs is the eighteenth-century *trompe-l'oeil* fresco (opposite) by Giacomo Lecchi in the ballroom of the Villa Lechi near Brescia.

Architectural Record, 1902

The Celestial

These odd structures of steps and multiple stairways, leading nowhere in particular, are playgrounds for sunbeams. A midsummer day's dream of Maharajah Jai Singh II (1686–1743), they are part of what were once the world's largest astronomical instruments at an observatory in Delhi. A statesman and city planner par excellence, Jai Singh was also a passionate astronomer. Distrusting the readings gained from small metal instruments, he thought to obtain greater accuracy by building gigantic enlargements of equinoctial sundials and assorted contraptions. If the results do not impress present-day astronomers, they put to shame the imagination of modern designers. The cluster below is composed of four instruments in one, called Misra Yantra. At left is the detail of another structure, one of two Jai Prakas, where the steps wind through what appear to be petrified friction gears. Opposite, part of the Samrat Yantra, or Supreme Instrument, rises from a murky pool—a stepmother giving birth to a litter of stairlets.

Familiar truths

By JOHN CANADAY

Thomas Eakins might well have been embittered when he painted his self-portrait (detail below), but there is no evidence of it here. The gaze is the clear, analytical one of an artist who was part scientist; the mouth belongs to a man incapable of either compromise or despair. Even his Spencerian signature (opposite) took an orderly place in his rational and realistic world; when he wished to sign it on the floor in a painting, he projected it (bottom) in correct perspective.

Thomas Eakins of Philadelphia, probably the greatest American painter and certainly one of the greatest nineteenth-century painters on any acceptable international list, was in his fifty-eighth year when he painted the self-portrait seen on this page. This was in 1902, and the painting was the "diploma" work required upon his election as Associate of the National Academy of Design. If he does not appear especially jubilant over his reception of this honor, one of a series of rather shamefaced recognitions that were to come to him during the remaining fourteen years of his life, the reason could be that during a long period of neglect he had discovered that there were not many people interested in listening to what he wanted to say as an artist.

As a supreme realist, Eakins appeared heavy and vulgar to a public that thought of art, and culture in general, largely in terms of a graceful sentimentality. Today he seems to us to have recorded his fellow Americans with a perception that was often as tender as it was vigorous, and to have preserved for us the essence of an American life which, indeed, he did not idealize—because it seemed to him beautiful beyond the necessity of idealization. Thus Eakins occupies a classical position in the history of nineteenth-century thought and art—that of the great man who saw too clearly in terms of the present to be acceptable to a public accustomed to thinking of greatness and beauty as prerogatives of the past, which therefore should be imitated.

And yet Eakins was not a modernist by today's standards, which have reversed the situation (we now have a public accustomed to thinking that great art exists only as a revolution against the past, which therefore must be rejected). In 1866, at the age of twenty-two, he was studying in Paris, where nascent impressionism, in the early work of Manet, was a roaring scandal. But he seems to have been indifferent to what was going on—even unaware of it, although he was alert and investigative by disposition. During Eakins's young manhood, impressionism fought its battles; during his mid-

in clear and beautiful language

Nature for Eakins was not a picturesque spectacle but an integral part of daily life. He was the first American artist to reveal urban man's relationship to nature other than sentimentally or nostalgically, and in these pictures his typical American figures are easily and harmoniously identified with familiar fields and waters.

The Swimming Hole, 1883

Mending the Net, 1881

Shad-Fishing at Gloucester on the Delaware, 1881

Max Schmitt in a Single Scull, 1871

Sailing, c. 1874

dle age, it won its decisive victories; during the last years of his life, cubism and Fauvism virtually changed the very definition of art. Throughout his life, Eakins stayed on course as a "scientific realist," a term applied to him (which he accepted), although it is incomplete because it fails to indicate the warmth of spirit that suffuses his art.

But the term is accurate as far as it goes, and the fact that it cannot be applied to any other major painter of the time is proof of the high degree of isolation of the art of this man who, paradoxically, loved the life around him and dedicated himself to recording it.

To whom can Eakins be compared, even among the realists who shared his half of the century? To Courbet? No; despite his credo of realism and his nominally common subjects, Courbet loved opulence and theatrical effects as dearly as any Salon painter. These effects Eakins detested. To Daumier? No, because this great humanitarian employed realism to probe a socio-political system that held no interest for Eakins. To Winslow Homer, who, as another American, might be closest? Not quite, since Homer, for all his close attention to the American scene, was more interested in discovering picturesqueness in the commonplace than in showing that the heart of life exists in everyday things. None of these men—not Courbet, because he lacked true sensitivity to any personality other than his own, and not Daumier or Homer, simply because they were not portraitists—left anything comparable to Eakins's characterizations of his contemporaries as individuals. His portraits, which in the end constitute his most impressive work, are a triumphant expression of the noblest ideal of his century, although certainly Eakins had no such ideal, no such program, in mind when he painted them.

It was the ideal of the average individual as an independent, responsible unit in society, living within a code of law and morals determined by himself and other individuals as a mass, yet remaining a free man within that mass. Even Daumier, who had a vast love for people that included full recognition of their foibles, never presented them to us as individuals but only as generic types. Eakins, even when confronted by a set of features utterly undistinguished, always managed to reproduce those features with surface exactitude while exploring the character of the individual who lived behind them.

This skill came to Eakins not quite by accident; it was

91

a secondary aspect of what he thought of as his main interest in art, his scientific realism. Portrait painting was a way of making a living; a lesser spirit would have been content to compromise with necessity by subjecting his talent to the creation of effigies that aimed to please—a compromise so nearly universal in the field of portraiture that it led John Singer Sargent, the most fashionable practitioner of his and Eakins's day, to comment that it was "a pimp's profession." But Eakins, apparently without setting himself a moral obligation, was temperamentally incapable of flattery. It is not surprising that some of the plain-faced people whom he painted with such unyielding truth were dissatisfied with the results and rejected their portraits, even though their posthumous (if undeserved) reward is that they have been immortalized; by comparison, most of Sargent's immortalizations now look like costume studies posed by manikins. Some of Eakins's sitters, on the other hand, committed a form of posthumous suicide by paying for a portrait they hated and then burning it.

Before saying much more about Eakins, we had better make some distinction between the terms "naturalism" and "realism," since both are applied to his art. The line between the two has never been well defined in painting, and they are often used interchangeably. But naturalism is a term specifically connected with the nineteenth century. More applicable to literature than to painting, naturalism signified an extreme of realism based on the methods of writers like Zola, who believed that the writer (or painter) could be and should be scientifically objective and precise in his description of life. Naturalism was not only anti-idealistic (it tended, pendulum fashion, to give more attention to the sordid than to the beautiful); it also tried to avoid all value judgments—something that is simply impossible for any writer or artist, since he cannot be an automaton.

Realism is less extreme. It may be anti-idealistic, since it regards the description of any facet of life as legitimate material for the artist, but it is also interpretive. If the realist does not idealize, he at least admits he responds. And by responding, he interprets according to his temperament.

In view of these definitions, hazy though they are, the description of Eakins as a scientific realist is quite accurate, if limited. His passion for anatomy and perspective as the bases for representation was indeed scientific and objective. But anatomy for him was also, and primarily, a way of understanding the human body, which he loved as the most beautiful of all natural objects. And perspective was a means of distilling from nature the essence of a world that delighted him. His art can be called naturalistic only in relative terms, only in comparison with the swooning romanticism that distorted the natural appearance of objects in the service of an extremely personal vision. Eakins was a realist in the most profound sense—a sane, practical, and reflective man who found that the mere fact of the existence of the world was beautiful in itself, and who asked no greater satisfaction than to observe it and to explore its structure.

This love of the world as one vast and glorious fact that could be explored, explained, and given its deepest meaning by discovering the physical principles that animated it, was at the heart of the nineteenth century's joy in science. It was also at the heart of Eakins's original interest in painting, so much so that at one time he hesitated between science and art as a profession. Where things are in perfect balance, a very small weight may be decisive on one side or another; Eakins's final choice of art may quite possibly have come about because his father, Benjamin Eakins, was a writing master who taught penmanship to young Philadelphia gentlefolk at a time when fine calligraphy, if not exactly thought of as an art, was cultivated and respected in very much the same way as drawing. There was a close bond between Thomas and his father; he liked to sign pictures in which his father appeared (including one of father and son hunting reedbirds in the marshes on the Cohansie River, across the Delaware from Philadelphia) BENJAMINI EAKINS FILIUS PINXIT.

Thomas, who was later to have three sisters, was born on July 25, 1844, the first child in this middle-class Scotch-Irish American family. When he was two years old, the family moved to a house at 1729 Mount Vernon Street, where he lived the rest of his life. However inconsequential in itself, the fact of this static residence is somehow an appropriate symbol of the solidity and continuity of an art that developed with such power in a single direction, during a time when restiveness, experiment, and various aesthetic alarums and excursions were typical of the lives of artists elsewhere. It is always surprising to remember that Eakins was almost an exact contemporary of Renoir, that he was only five years younger than Cézanne and only nine years older than Van Gogh.

If the relation of vital statistics to the sequence of aesthetic revolutions meant anything, we would have to say that Eakins lagged a generation, maybe two generations, behind the greatest of his European contemporaries. But Eakins's insensibility to the revolutionary sequence is evidence enough that American culture was not then of a character (let us not say "was too far behind") to nourish these revolutions even if they had been imported as they occurred. It was a culture which had produced so few artists it could call truly its own that it still needed the kind of painter Eakins was. He was one of those whose strength lies in their revelation of ways of thinking and feeling that are born and bred into them by their time and place, as opposed to the clairvoyants or prophets whose strength is that they speak in the strange tongues of genius.

In Eakins's America, technical conservatism was not only a valid means of expression but the *only* valid one for an indigenously expressive art. The adoption of impressionist techniques at that stage of the game, not to mention post-

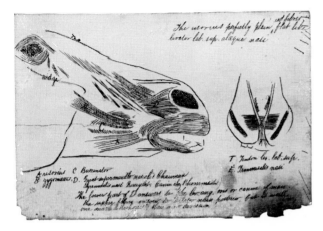

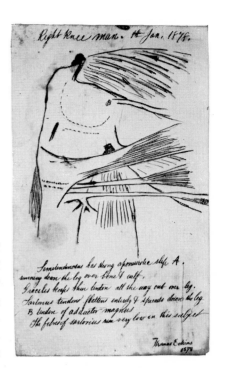

As an anatomist Eakins made comparative dissection drawings of men and horses (right and left), and published a study, "The Differential Action of Certain Muscles Passing More Than One Joint." As a mathematician he reduced "complicated things . . . to simple things" by geometrical perspective as in the precisely plotted and meticulously drawn sketch below—which, transferred to canvas in 1872, became the oil The Pair-Oared Shell.

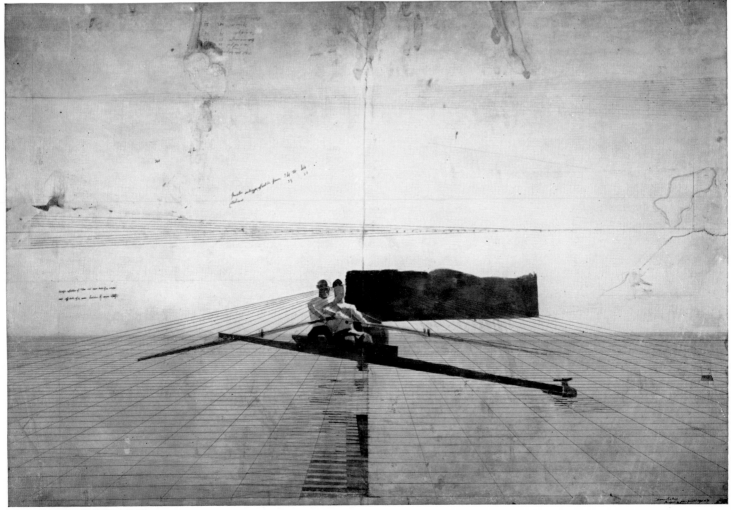

In 1884 Eakins collaborated with the pioneer of serial-action photography, Eadweard Muybridge, in making some studies of nude athletes in motion. Not satisfied with Muybridge's battery of twenty-four cameras, Eakins devised a single camera with revolving disks, thus anticipating the principle of the motion-picture camera.

impressionism, would have been a kind of anachronism-in-advance. Eakins's trouble with the public and his patrons came not because he painted in a way that people in general did not understand (this was the impressionists' trouble in France), but because he painted in a way that they understood perfectly. There was no question as to what he was saying or how he was saying it; he was speaking in clear (and beautiful) language about familiar truths, but for this very reason he offended people who had become accustomed to the idea that the painter's function was to speak in the debased rhetoric of the Salon, which confused truth with sentimental clichés. The impressionists had to fight this same battle, but their manner of assault differed as their terrain was Paris instead of Philadelphia, New York, or Boston.

And yet in spite of their contrasting surfaces—the impressionists with their broken, sparkling color and their forms so frequently eroded by effects of light and air, and Eakins with his firm definition and, sometimes, the brown shadowy depths so abominated by his French contemporaries—Eakins and the impressionists were close kin. Both painted a bourgeois world that put its faith in mundane, practical values. In the hands of the academicians these values, disguised as idealism, bred some of the most flatly prosaic and banal art of all time. But the great realists of the century—the impressionists were their consummation in France and Eakins was their sole indisputably great man in America—embraced the everyday world and loved it for the way it

looked, felt, tasted, sounded, and smelled. They found it worth loving in spite of all the confusion and ordinariness because, if you knew how to hunt it out, there was something firm and wonderful in daily life that made all the trivialities and accidents worthwhile.

In France, where artistic revolutions had been following one another not only by generations but by split generations, the new technical vocabulary of impressionism was a natural accompaniment to a new way of revealing the world. Not only in color, but in the ways of putting a picture together, the impressionists went beyond anything that an American could then absorb without becoming, as Mary Cassatt eventually became, an adopted citizen of a foreign culture.

All that has changed; we are accustomed now to an internationalism in art that jumps the Atlantic, in both directions, as one experimental movement succeeds another. Eakins preceded a generation of painters who began to take up the slack, but he seems less to have resisted foreign influences than to have been simply impervious to them.

Eakins belonged to the last generation of American artists for whom a truly indigenous expression was possible, except in the limited terms of folk art in the hinterlands. The country's increasing international power and international involvement, culminating in the First World War, so changed its character that for an artist to be American in the way that Eakins was American became impossible. His death on June

Eakins's pictures of boxers, rowers, and wrestlers (right) were his solution to the problem of representing nudes, or at least partial nudes, realistically. Even as a student he drew the body (below) not as an object of artificial grace but as an organism where beauty of form meant beauty of structural function.

PHILADELPHIA MUSEUM OF ART

25, 1916, less than ten months before our entry into the war, was a coincidence of timing that is almost symbolic. After 1918, American*ism*—and the last syllable is the important one—could only be a form of isolationism, an artificial and reactionary attitude toward painting that had its temporary victory and final defeat in the regionalist art of the 1930's, at the same time that a group of American politicians, the isolationists, were trying to make a walled island of the United States.

But Eakins had come into his young manhood with the Civil War; the decisive years of his development as an artist were the decades of the nineteenth century that brought this country truly of age, that determined its character as something more than a hybrid, part pioneer and part, if vestigially, colonial. During Eakins's best years—the years of early maturity, when an artist's direction is set for him—European manners in art were still regarded as imported refinements that artists might aspire to, but this aspiration was a denial of more spontaneous and hence more specifically American ways of expression.

The impressionists, who shared with Eakins a faith in the commonplace as a natural source of inspiration, would certainly have recognized their kinship with him if they could have known him. They would surely have recognized his stature, and just as surely his contrasting Americanness—his solidity, his trust in factual clarity. Any provincial flavor in his conservative technique was inherent in the true ex-

pression of a culture that had not yet questioned itself at base, and hence did not stimulate its artists to question the efficacy of traditional art forms.

For an aristocratic and Europeanized intellectual such as Henry James (Eakins's exact contemporary), the European-American contrast seemed a cultural hiatus in fashions and manners that was anguishing to someone who loved both worlds. But Eakins, never a fashionable man and by James's standards not even a well-educated one, could remain undivided. Lately we have come, almost without realizing it, to equate the importance of any nineteenth-century artist with the degree to which he was a prophet or a forebear of modernism. But Eakins's strength lies in the fact that he was not a prophet and not even interested in following the latest thing. Prophecy and fashion, which in the art of painting mean experiment and embellishment, went against the grain of Eakins's vision of a world so inexhaustibly beautiful and meaningful from day to day that a painter need only (to use Eakins's own word) "re-create" what he saw to fulfill his function as interpreter.

As a sturdy young boy, Eakins had loved the rural countryside around Philadelphia, where he boated, fished, and hunted. He attended Central High School, an institution that was, and is, notable in the Philadelphia public school system for educating the brightest boys at a level several hefty notches above that of the average high school. He was an exceptional student there, strongest in mathematics and science. He was also good at art, at a time when art was taught by rule and not regarded as a form of *laissez faire* for self-expression. Mechanical drawing and perspective, which of course are forms of geometry, were as important or more important than sketching. No artist since the Renaissance, when its rules were being formulated, has been more interested in pure perspective than Eakins was. Some of his preliminary perspective studies for paintings have an analytical clarity that makes them appealing to contemporary eyes as independent works of abstract art.

Without these early analytical and scientific associations, art would probably not have interested Eakins as a profession, and his first enthusiasm for his tentative choice was a bit dampened at the Pennsylvania Academy of the Fine Arts in Philadelphia, which he entered in 1861 when he was seventeen. The introductory year, standard in art schools at the time, consisted almost entirely of copying plaster casts of antique sculptures, a meticulous discipline teaching a few principles that any gifted student can pick up quickly.

Drawing from casts has discouraged many talents, stultified others, and delayed the development of virtually all who have been subjected to it. At best, it inculcates an ideal of anemic grace in its substitution of the smooth, blank forms of inaccurate casts for the vitally idealized originals of antiquity. This warped introduction to classical art may explain why Eakins during all his life never came to an understanding of it. Although he revered the Parthenon figures, he thought they were "undoubtedly modeled from life," a misconception of their reference to life as a source. He said that "nature is just as varied and just as beautiful in our day as she was in the time of Phidias," and also that there could be no objection to idealization as long as one "understands what it is that he is idealizing." This last, of course, was the point, but by every evidence of his work, Eakins continued to think of idealization as a form of watering-down, as indeed it was in the hands of his contemporaries.

The hours and days of waste and boredom in the cast-drawing classes were punctuated at the Academy by occasional life classes. Although the nude body was regarded as little more than a living cast that could be shifted into a few standard poses, Eakins's earliest drawings from life are full of weight, structure, and a potential for movement. The human body had already become for him the most wonderful thing in the world—not an evocation of sensuous delights or a symbol of fecundity, as it became for Renoir in those same years; and not a rather curious, even unlovely, object that somehow could take on and reveal the social and psychological status of an individual, as it became for Degas; and not even the most fluid and adjustable compositional element available to an artist, as it had been for centuries to any number of painters. For Eakins, the body was an organism so wonderfully articulated and interdependent in all its parts that nothing could equal its beauty as the one greatest single object in the whole of creation.

This was a scientist's recognition of fact as the truest miracle, the most fascinating mystery of all because it can be explained, and because its fascination increases as the mystery is unraveled. During his years as an art student, Eakins supplemented the Academy classes with courses in anatomy and dissection, which included witnessing operations, at The Jefferson Medical College. He even considered becoming a surgeon.

After following this divided course for five years, he made his final decision in 1866 and went to Paris to study at the *Ecole des Beaux-Arts,* where all drawing and painting was based on the nude. In many ways this is the most contradictory period, or the only contradictory period, in his life. His master was Jean Léon Gérôme, a superb technician but an artist who now seems as stuffy and artificial a painter as any the Salon produced. Yet, in spite of Eakins's abomination of affectation, he admired not only Gérôme but some other Salon painters who would seem unlikely to appeal to him. He did reject, significantly, painters like Bouguereau, whose female nudes, while impeccably drawn, were so candy-tinted and coy that even a young American excited by his first study in Paris could not fail to recognize them as unrelated to the reality that he had already investigated by dissection.

What seems most curious, at first, is that Eakins showed

TEXT CONTINUED ON PAGE 105

American Faces

A Portfolio in Gravure

Eakins did not think of himself primarily as a portrait painter, but his portraits—mostly done for his own pleasure—make up the best group in American art. Since commissions were few (his portraits did not flatter), Eakins asked friends and members of his family to pose in the studio he set up on the top floor of his father's house. At his death the studio was filled with these remarkable likenesses, some of which HORIZON *reproduces—in full or in detail—in this gravure portfolio. Amelia C. Van Buren (opposite) was an artist who had been in Eakins's classes at the Pennsylvania Academy. He painted her about 1891, in the dark years after his rupture with that institution. This may well be the finest of all American portraits.*

The eminent surgeon Dr. John H. Brinton sat for his friend Eakins in 1876. Brinton had served with Grant, was teaching at Philadelphia's Jefferson Medical College (where Eakins studied anatomy), and would eventually succeed to the chair of Dr. Gross (opposite). His rugged face is that of a scholar, a man of conscience and reflection, and a successful man of the world—and so Eakins painted him, rather than as the towering near-divinity that he made of Gross.

The Gross Clinic (detail); THE JEFFERSON MEDICAL COLLEGE AND MEDICAL MUSEUM

Eakins painted The Gross Clinic, *his most ambitious figure composition, in the hope of exhibiting it at the Centennial Exposition of 1876. The central figure of Dr. Samuel David Gross, and especially the powerful head, is more than an accurate portrait; it has become a symbol of the scientific intellect. Despite that, the picture as a whole was considered too "indelicate" for a mixed public. Eakins finally got it into the medical exhibit, and sold it for 200 dollars.*

OVERLEAF: *Music, as a communion between friends, played a large part in Eakins's life. The pianist in* The Pathetic Song *(left) is his pupil Susan Hannah Macdowell, whom he married in 1884. The* Concert Singer *(right) was Weda Cook, who was a friend of Walt Whitman and who set his "O Captain! My Captain!" to music. The conductor's hand is also a portrait of sorts: it was posed for by Charles M. Schmidtz, conductor of the old Germania Orchestra.*

Mrs. Letitia Wilson Jordan Bacon (detail); IN THE BROOKLYN MUSEUM COLLECTION

The subject of this portrait of 1888, Mrs. Letitia Bacon, was the sister of a pupil and close friend of Eakins. The painter saw her at a party and asked her to pose for him in the dress she was wearing (at parties Eakins often stared at possible female sitters so fixedly that he made them uncomfortable). He liked to paint handsome women and he enjoyed translating the textures of fine clothing to canvas, but he was utterly incapable of depicting mere idealized prettiness.

102

This 1900 portrait of Mrs. Frishmuth, a Philadelphia collector of musical instruments, shows Eakins at his painterly best. The head is more than a masterly reproduction of a set of extraordinary features: it is the depiction of a determined, reflective intelligence. Together, the portraits of Mrs. Bacon (opposite) and Mrs. Frishmuth show the range of Eakins's mastery of characterization without exaggeration, as well as his ability to reveal and proclaim the sitter's personality.

OVERLEAF: Girl with a Cat, Eakins's first large portrait, is exceptional for its tender, romantic mood. It shows his first fiancée, Katherine Crowell, in 1872; the chair is the same in which Miss Van Buren posed (see page 97) some twenty years later. Katherine was the sister of a boyhood friend, William J. Crowell, who later married the eldest of Eakins's three sisters. Katherine Crowell died in her early twenties, and Eakins did not marry until he was forty.

TIME TO STUMP THE EXPERTS

From left to right, "regulars" Oscar Levant, John Kieran, and the late F.P.A. with guest Jan Struthers, an author who died in 1953.

By JOHN KIERAN

*The questions were hard.
The answers were erudite. But above all
the panelists—singly or collectively,
quietly or uproariously—were funny.
This was the unbeatable formula
that, in pretelevision days, attracted
millions of Americans to
their radios once a week for ten years*

During the decade from 1938 to 1948, a cheerful voice over the radio announcing that it was now time to "stump the experts" meant only one thing to some ten million Americans. It meant that "Information Please" was about to go on the air, and that we could anticipate a half-hour of delight. Those of us who were devotees were astonished at the panelists' expertise, and were frequently convulsed by their wit. By the thousands we sent in questions, hoping that ours would be chosen for use on the show, and those of us who were particularly astute, or lucky, received Encyclopaedia Britannicas—cheerfully dealt out when the experts failed to come up with the correct answers.

John Kieran, at that time a well-known sports columnist for The New York Times *and on the side a devoted naturalist, was one of the original panelists, and he stuck with the program through its ten years of existence. In the following article he fondly recalls the history of that durable, literate, and uniquely charming radio show. This material will appear in slightly different form in Mr. Kieran's new book, an autobiography entitled* Not Under Oath, *to be published in October by Houghton Mifflin.*

One day in May, 1938, my desk phone rang. The man at the other end said that his name was Dan Golenpaul and he invited me to go on a radio show. I thanked him and said that I wasn't interested. The man kept talking, telling me that his was a panel show, that questions came in from the public and the members of the panel tried to answer them. A great many questions on sports came from younger listeners and he needed somebody to cover that field. He told me that Franklin P. Adams, the noted wit and author of the newspaper column "The Conning Tower," had recommended me. I asked him to thank Mr. Adams for the compliment but I still was not interested.

The caller became irritated. He informed me that I was no great attraction and that there were far more famous sports writers available. To this I agreed cheerfully and suggested that he invite one of them to go on his show. This irritated him further but he kept on talking. I couldn't shake him off. Finally he said almost in a rage: "Couldn't you even give this thing a half-hour trial?

"When?"

"Tomorrow morning, eleven o'clock, here at NBC."

The man had worn me down. More to get rid of him than anything else, I agreed to show up the next morning. It could be done on my way to the office and that would be the last of it.

The appointment was kept in one of the big studios on the third floor at NBC, and there I found Dan Golenpaul and members of his staff, various radio executives and technicians, and some other candidates who were to be tested out as possible members of the panel. Clifton Fadiman was there. He was the master of ceremonies and read the questions when the show was on the air, which it had been once a week for three or four weeks past. That was why they were seeking new panelists. They had discovered that not all the starting quartet could go the distance. For one thing, only Franklin P. Adams of the original four knew or cared anything about sports, and even he knew only tennis, baseball, and the football fortunes of his alma mater, the University of Michigan. Somebody had to fill the gap, and that was where I was to come in.

The names of the others who sat through the half-hour of questioning that morning do not come to mind. All I remember is that I had fun sitting there and speaking up when I knew the answers to the questions. At the end of the session Mr. Golenpaul came up to me and the conversation went something like this:

"Was that hard to take?"

"No, it was a lot of fun."

"Well, will you go on the air with us?"

"When?"

"Friday night at eight-thirty."

"Where?"

"Right here in this studio."

"I'll be here."

"We're on a budget now—sustaining. Until we get a sponsor, all I can give you is forty dollars for each show."

"That's all right with me."

I didn't add that I would have gone on for nothing, which was exactly what I had been paid for previous performances on the air and the reason why I had not jumped at another invitation when Dan Golenpaul first mentioned the topic over the phone.

Thus I became a member of the panel of the "Information Please" radio program that became nationally popular in a matter of months and catapulted its regulars into public notice, where we remained for more than a decade. I may be prejudiced —I'm sure I am—in saying that it was the most literate popular entertainment program ever to go on radio or television.

Aside from any contribution that I made to it, we had in Clifton Fadiman and Franklin P. Adams two of the brightest of the contemporary literary set, and in Oscar Levant, who joined us shortly after I made the team, a young man of remarkable musical talent and a positive genius for making offhand cutting remarks that couldn't have been sharper if he had honed them in his mind for a week. Oscar was with us every other time. When he was present, we had one guest to make up our panel of four. When he was absent, we had two guests.

Until Dan Golenpaul came along with his format for "Information Please," the popular quiz shows on radio featured a glib master of ceremonies directing questions at volunteer victims on a stage or at persons picked at random from a studio audience. Anyone who answered a question correctly was suitably rewarded. "Thirty silver dollars to the lady with the flowered hat!" or "Give that gentleman in the gallery twelve silver dollars!" The studio audience cheered. That part of it was jolly enough. But too often the exposure of the utter ignorance of the persons to whom comparatively simple questions were put was embarrassing. The Golenpaul scheme was to reverse that process. Have the public direct questions at persons who might be reasonably expected to give a good answer.

Thus the first order of business when we went on the air each week was a recital by Clifton Fadiman of "how we play the game." Listeners could send in questions on anything under the sun. If the question was used, the sender would receive a copy of the *Encyclopaedia Britannica World Atlas.* If the question "stumped the experts," the sender would receive in addition the twenty-four volume set of the *Encyclopaedia Britannica* and, through the war years, a fifty-dollar war bond. The sender of any question had to include his own idea of the correct answer—or answers in case the question was divided into different parts, as most of them were.

On multiple-part questions the panelists usually were required to "get three out of four" or perhaps "four out of five," but if we hadn't been giving away enough sets of the encyclopaedia, Mr. Fadiman would calmly change that to "get all on this," or even strain a point to call a decision against us and in favor of the sender of the question.

What quickly made the program exceptional was the quality of the guests who were persuaded to appear on the panel. They came because the show was literate as well as consistently entertaining. They expected to enjoy themselves and most of them did. We had famous authors, college presidents and professors, United States senators and representatives, members of the President's cabinet, governors and mayors, top scientists, and in the old-fashioned phrase of those days, "stars of stage, screen, and radio." Wendell Willkie first caught the attention of the general public by his apt and genial answers when he was a guest on our program, and added much to his popularity when he appeared with us in two movie shorts of "Information Please." Indeed, the release of the first of these films, while Willkie was trying to get the Republican nomination for President in the late spring of 1940, won him such favorable comment that Ed Flynn, Democratic political boss and attorney for the movie company that was distributing the films, kept the second one off the screen until after the November election. Not that it would have made any difference, but politicians never take a chance if they can help it.

It is necessary to explain all this now because, just as in Egypt there arose a king who knew not Joseph, since "Information Please" went over the hill there has arisen a whole generation that never heard the program or saw the films, which, incidentally, were burned to death in a warehouse fire on New York's West Side. Brought up on a spate of quite different types of quiz shows featuring giveaway gambling and even criminal skulduggery, this younger generation could have no idea of the intelligent entertainment offered by our show and the innocent merriment it generated for listeners of all ages across the country. Getting the right guests was the most important part of the production. Giving a right answer was the least important contribution by any guest or regular on the panel. It was generally more fun when the answer was wrong, especially if the culprit tried to wriggle out of it. An uproarious error or a brilliant bit of irrelevance was rated far above any dull delivery of truth.

It was Clifton Fadiman, of course, who kept things stirred up when we were on the air. He was perfect in the part of master of ceremonies for such a program—cultured, witty, and perfectly poised. Quick on the trigger, too. He was never thrown for a loss

NO COACHING REQUIRED

Pittsburgh Post-Gazette

"Information Please" was so well known that cartoonists could safely assume that a picture showing a moderator and four panelists would evoke the proper image in almost any context. Listeners, too, as on the following pages, were reliable subjects for gags. Directly below is a musical interlude by Fred Allen, left, and F.P.A. The bottom photograph was taken during a wartime USO tour. The uniformed cast includes, from left to right, F.P.A., Beatrice Lillie, Kieran, Reginald Gardiner, and Clifton Fadiman.

DAN GOLENPAUL ASSOCIATES

DAN GOLENPAUL ASSOCIATES

by an unexpected answer—and we had some dazzlers, most of them from Oscar Levant, a composer who was never composed. Oscar couldn't sit still. He fidgeted. He shuffled his feet, drummed his fingers on the table, hummed under his breath, and whistled softly between his teeth. One night he answered a question on botany correctly. It stunned the studio audience. It stunned me, too. I was the one who was expected to answer questions in natural history. This led to a brisk debate on one occasion.

A listener had sent in a question on the average life-span of different creatures. Ordinarily such questions and the answers that came with them were checked for accuracy by the "Information Please" staff, but apparently the office library had no book containing figures on such life expectancies and the card reached Mr. Fadiman's hands with the sender's figures intact. There were four or five parts to the question. Since little is known about the life-span of creatures in the wild, all I could do was guess. Mr. Fadiman, consulting his card, called each of my guesses wrong.

The sharpest dissent was over the average life-span of the downy woodpecker. Because of predators, storms, parasites, and other avian plagues, most of our small birds lead short and not necessarily merry lives. I put the average life-span of the downy woodpecker at perhaps three years, certainly not more than five. Mr. Fadiman informed me, on the authority of the card he held in his hand, that the average downy woodpecker pounded tree trunks for twenty-three years before it shuffled off this mortal coil. I informed Mr. Fadiman, without consulting any card, that this was a lot of applesauce and asked him how many downy woodpeckers of that age he knew. Thus challenged, he admitted that he had no personal acquaintance with downy woodpeckers of any age and would defer decision on the whole question for a week, pending investigation.

I spent that week thumbing reference books on the subject and consulting my friends at the Bronx Zoo and the American Museum of Natural History. The experts I consulted agreed unanimously that the life-spans Mr. Fadiman had on his card were ridiculous and they wondered where they had been manufactured. It turned out that the sender of the question had gleaned his answers from a "filler paragraph" in an almanac stuffed with articles on astrology and studded with illustrated advertisements for patent medicines. The decision on the appeal was a verdict for me by the whole court. The sender of the question received an atlas but not a single volume of the *Encyclopaedia Britannica*.

There were no other pitched battles over the facts of life on the program, but I remember challenging another official answer because it dealt with a matter of spelling that always raised my body temperature. The question concerned one of the minor horrors of war, the way English and American soldiers in Europe mispronounced the names of cities and towns on the Continent. Ypres, for instance, was "Wipers" to the British tommies in Belgium in World War I. I have forgotten the other sections of the question, but what stirred me up was Mr. Fadiman's request for the proper spelling and French pronunciation of the city that our soldiers referred to as "Reems." I put my hand up and so did Mr. Adams. He was called upon and spelled out the name of the city in six letters: R–H–E–I–M–S.

"Right," said Mr. Fadiman. "Now, give us the French pronunciation."

Mr. Adams made a stab at it and I winced.

"Don't you like his pronunciation?" Mr. Fadiman asked me.

"I don't even like his spelling."

Mr. Fadiman, who knew French and had spent a year in Paris as a postgraduate student, was taken aback. He asked what was wrong with the spelling. I said that the French spelled it "Reims," with no "h" in it. Mr. Fadiman seemed doubtful. He looked at his card. It read "Rheims" and he said so. I suggested that he look at the label of any bottle of champagne from the Reims district. He said that he had no such bottle on him at the moment but would gladly inspect one if I would provide it after the show.

Musical questions probably gave our listeners more cause for laughter than any topics with which we tangled. Oscar Levant answered most of them, and Oscar was always good for a bright response edged with acid. F.P.A. knew all the old popular ballads and had Gilbert and Sullivan by heart. I began playing the piano by ear when I was five years old and have kept it up relentlessly ever since, despite some protests from the strangest places—musical circles, for instance. One night Oscar Levant came into the studio while I was filling in some idle time on the piano and, after listening a moment, said: "Ha! He's playing the Melody in F in F sharp!"

Guilty as charged. It was the only way I could play it at all. Our staff pianist, who was with us throughout our years on the air, was Joe Kahn, who was also the regular pianist for the NBC Orchestra, which had been assembled to perform under the baton of that maestro of maestros, Arturo Toscanini. Joe's customary chore was to play a few bars or a short passage from some opus, and our problem was to name the piece or the composer—or perhaps we were requested to sing the chorus of an old song after Joe had played the verse.

The most striking of all the answers about music came in response to a question that wasn't even on the card. That perfect gentleman and pluperfect pianist, Artur Rubinstein, was one of the two guests that evening, and at one point Joe Kahn played brief passages from great piano compositions and it was up to Artur, who appeared with us half a dozen times at least, to identify the source of each excerpt and name the composer. One short, fast passage baffled him. He thought it over, shook his head, and gave up. Reading from the card, Mr. Fadiman named the work and the composer.

"Ah, yes," said Mr. Rubinstein, "it's a piece you don't often hear—but I should have recognized it."

After announcing that a set of the *Encyclopaedia Britannica* would go to the questioner who had "stumped the experts," Mr. Fadiman went on cheerfully: "Well, we missed that one, but I think we can all agree that our studio pianist, Mr. Kahn, played the passage very well. Wouldn't you say so, Mr. Rubinstein?"

The maestro considered the matter for perhaps half a second and then said firmly: "No!"

On a national hookup! The studio audience roared with laughter. Kip Fadiman, when he managed to stop laughing himself, said: "That's a conversation stopper if I ever heard one."

By that time Mr. Rubinstein was as embarrassed as his innocent victim, Joe Kahn, but nothing could be done about it. The critical word had been heard from coast to coast. We went on to the next question.

Of course we understood, and so did Joe Kahn and anybody who knew anything about music. There was Joe sitting at a piano on a stage, waiting to jump into short and complicated passages from difficult pieces of music. In each case and at a given signal he was to begin nowhere and end nowhere, so to speak. Nobody could be expected to play such bits perfectly. Artur Rubinstein said he couldn't. That was enough to mollify Joe Kahn, who had recovered quickly from his state of shock.

There were no other musical crises on the program that I recall except one where I flunked out because I was armed with

© 1941 THE NEW YORKER MAGAZINE, INC.

"Oh, Willard, 'Information Please' is on."

the wrong instrument. That evening the panel consisted of F.P.A., Oscar, Ethel Barrymore, and the then sports columnist of *The New York Times* whose name escapes me for the moment. We had to be on our guard against trick questions like "How far can a Bombay duck fly?" The answer is: as far as you can throw it. Bombay duck is a fish curry dish served in India. Or another question might be: "In what part of your house would you put a set of Napier's Tables if somebody gave them to you?" On the bookshelf; they are tables of logarithms. On the musical side it might be: "The name of what opera might be construed as a command to a man to speak out?" *William Tell*! Or "What familiar operatic aria might a milkman warble in praise of his wares?" Answer—hold on to your hat—"Ah, So Pure" from *Martha*. Often the panelist might be required to sing or whistle part of the answer to prove that he really knew the music.

The questions just presented were mere inventions of my disordered mind, but they give you an idea of what we could expect when we sat down and faced Mr. Fadiman on the other side of the stage. I don't remember the question that brought the instrumental music into play the night Ethel Barrymore was with us, but the accepted answer was the title of a popular song that all of us knew. "Play it together!" commanded Mr. Fadiman. It was a surprise to us but not to the stagehands. An extra piano was on the platform that night. Oscar took that. Joe Kahn gallantly yielded his piano to Miss Barrymore. A page boy who sneaked up from behind handed Franklin P. Adams a harmonica, on which he fancied himself a virtuoso, and another page boy deposited a full-sized piano accordion beside my chair. The others started off without waiting for me: by the time I had lifted the instrument, worked my arms through the straps, and settled myself comfortably in harness, the others were playing the closing chords of the musical offering. I never sounded a note, which was probably all for the best.

It usually is somebody else who brings it up, but when it is mentioned, I am inclined to boast of the guest list we had on

© 1940 THE NEW YORKER MAGAZINE, INC.

"All right, you're smarter than John Kieran. Let it go at that."

"Information Please." In the decade that we were on the air it ran to more than four hundred notables of one sort or another, many of whom enjoyed themselves so much that they frequently came back for more. The repeaters included two men from the Commonwealth's diplomatic corps, Britain's Sir Gladwyn Jebb, and Canada's Lester B. Pearson, Ellis Arnall, the melodious Governor of Georgia, Bea Lillie, Raymond Massey, Fred Allen, and at least half a dozen members of what is reputed to be the most exclusive club in the world, the United States Senate. After a few daring celebrities took the plunge and came on the program, the rush was on. Everybody was eager to get into the act. Being a guest on "Information Please" became a badge of distinction, the equivalent of being tapped for skill and brains.

The only problem the radio success of "Information Please" brought to the regular panelists was a flood of personal mail that grew heavier with the steadily increasing popularity of the program. Each of us received endless invitations to deliver lectures, contribute articles gratis to college and high-school publications, make speeches at breakfasts, luncheons, and dinners in honor of somebody or something, and do volunteer work for countless good causes. Because I answered most of the questions on natural history, I had additional requests to lead nature walks, talk to garden clubs, identify from written descriptions thereof birds, beasts, and reptiles that never existed by land, sea, or air, and give expert advice by return mail on the care and feeding of sick parakeets, tame turtles, pet alligators, tropical fish, and other assorted livestock around the house.

Turning out a daily sports column for *The Times* had been a fair-sized job in itself. I had also written a few books and many magazine articles on the side before the radio program skyrocketed us into public notice. In short, I had enough to keep me busy before this flood of mail came pouring down on me. Emergency measures were necessary. All those letters deserved appreciative answers.

To solve the problem I took on a part-time secretary, a good boy in the office who was a fast and accurate stenographer. For him I drew up a list of form letters that would serve as polite answers to my correspondents. Most of them were firm declinations with many thanks for the honor of the invitation. Thus I could glance at a letter, get the gist of it, and toss it to the boy with the remark "No speech," "No article," "Contract forbids it," "Ask the Museum of Natural History," or simply "Don't know." Some letters were so completely baffling that no one of the stock answers would do. For these special cases I devised a letter to be written and signed by the boy himself as my secretary. I have forgotten the exact wording, but I remember that I rather prided myself on it at the time. Beyond a courteous acknowledgement that the letter had been received, it was a plea in avoidance of a direct answer coupled with a hint that Mr. Kieran was not in the best of health at the moment and couldn't go into the matter. The code phrase for that answer was "Mister Kieran is dead."

Handling correspondence in this fashion solved some of the problems that came with the success of our radio show, but not all of them. A man called up one day and threatened to take legal action because I hadn't acknowledged receipt of his letter containing valuable material of some kind. I had no recollection of any such letter as he described. He insisted that it was a very important letter and I must have received it. I replied that I was an unimportant person and had never received an important letter in my life. I gained the impression that he believed only the first half of my declaration. But he took no legal action.

There were, of course, invitations that had to be accepted. They went with the well-paid job. You had to write articles or speak or just put in appearances at luncheons or dinners for charity, art, or education. Most of it was pleasant enough, but my life was becoming too crowded. I was a sports columnist, a writer on natural history, and a radio performer. I was hurrying in three directions at once.

At this point things got worse. We began to make movie

shorts of "Information Please." Up to that time we had been only voices in the night and nobody recognized us on the street the next day. But when the films began appearing on movie screens from Broadway to the Golden Gate, our faces were exposed to public view and we were in for trouble. In no time at all we were being halted by strangers who had something to say about the program or our parts in it. Usually the stranger began by stating frankly: "I have a question that will stump you." Almost every time the stranger was right.

There was one week when three different "Information Please" shorts were running in Broadway movie houses. That was when I gave up eating lunch alone in any downtown restaurant or hotel. Some stranger was sure to sit down at my table and either toss a question at me, invite me to join a society, ask me to speak at the annual breakfast, luncheon, or dinner of some organization, or try to persuade me that astrology and dowsing are the only exact sciences known to man. Worse than spoiling my lunch or dinner, this sort of thing cut into my reading hours. I always went about with a book in my pocket and pulled it out when I sat down in a bus or a subway car. You can get in two acts of *Hamlet* or thirty pages of *La Rôtisserie de la Reine Pédauque* between Times Square and 242nd Street on the Van Cortlandt Park line. But not when strangers recognize you and come over to discuss Shakespeare and the musical glasses.

Of course I realized that those who wrote or spoke to me were the radio followers whose interest in the program made possible the salaries we were getting for going on the air, probably the easiest money anybody ever earned. I always tried to be polite to strangers who came up and spoke to me, and I answered every letter that bore a legible name and address.

In June of 1948, after a run of ten consecutive years as one one of the top shows on radio, "Information Please" vanished into thin air. It was Dan Golenpaul's choice. The sponsor was willing to go back on the air in the autumn at the same price, but with a Presidential election coming up and business conditions for the future uncertain, he didn't want to sign for a long term. Dan wouldn't settle for anything short of a two-year contract and, when he didn't get it, he withdrew the show. I was sorry because it was always a lot of fun, but I didn't feel at all that "Othello's occupation's gone." I had plenty of other work to keep me busy.

About this time Dan Golenpaul had us working sporadically on a plan to put "Information Please" on television via film, and we made a few pilot films for exhibition to the trade. To me, they seemed much like the old movie shorts that were lost to posterity by fire except that, to my regret, we didn't have the original cast of characters. Most important of all, we had lost our incomparable master of ceremonies, Clifton Fadiman. After years of bickering over matters of which I knew nothing, he and Dan had parted without tears. Oscar Levant had settled down— if you could call it that—in Beverly Hills and was unavailable, even if Dan had wanted him, which I doubt. They, too, had enjoyed a falling out.

That left only F.P.A. and me of the original four. Half a loaf may be better than no bread, but you can't cut everything as fine as that. Half a team can't function as well as a whole team, and half a horse wouldn't get anywhere in racing. Some of our old friends showed up at the studios for these pilot films, and we enjoyed the company of newer celebrities, like Sarah Churchill and Alistair Cooke, but the problems of staging and filming the show for television never reached any happy solution and eventually the whole thing bogged down.

At the end—and it really was the end—"Information Please" went on live television as a summer replacement for the Fred Waring show in 1952. By that time Franklin P. Adams was in such poor shape physically that he had to retire after the first telecast. Kip Fadiman, who had happily rejoined us for this series of programs, left his emcee chair in the middle of the summer. Either he took himself off or Mr. Golenpaul took him off; I never knew which. Thus I became the only survivor of the original quartet, and I mightily missed the others. Furthermore, it was most difficult to get guest stars of note for the program in the sweltering summer in New York City. Those who could afford it stayed away in horror. Thus the shows that we put on lacked the zest and sparkle of the ancient days of radio. I was not surprised when there came no insistent demand for more of "Information Please" on television after Fred Waring and his Pennsylvanians came back to claim their own on Sunday nights.

Looking back across the years, it seems to me that four things were responsible for the rapid rise and the long period of popularity of "Information Please" on radio. Dan Golenpaul supplied three of them. The first was the bright idea of turning the quiz program of those days in the opposite direction. Get rid of the slick professional asking stammering or stupefied innocent victims inane questions. Get a panel of professional men and let them be the targets of ardent amateur questioners. Thus the listening audience is part and parcel of the game. Any listener in this country might win a set of the *Encyclopaedia Britannica*.

The second important item was the quality of the guest list. The list was imposing—top figures in all the fields of human endeavor: art, science, literature, education, sports, music, theatre, and public life. Dan Golenpaul tried for the best and snared a great many of them.

The third ingredient supplied by Dan Golenpaul was the integrity of the program. It was honest. With the contestants involved, it couldn't be anything else. More than that, the unexpected and even uninhibited answers to many of the questions proved to the millions of listeners that the performance was truly "spontaneous and unrehearsed" as advertised.

The last, and perhaps the crowning touch, was the arch urbanity and literate lightness with which master of ceremonies Clifton Fadiman handled the show on the air, the regulars on the panel, the honored guests—and the unexpected answers! As for my part in it, I feel as certain old ball players must feel who wore the flannels of the New York Yankees of 1927. It was wonderful to have been on such a team.

The pontificate of Angelo Roncalli, Pope John XXIII, was brief, but it will be long remembered—not only for John's great achievements but for his infectious, kindly, and disarming wit. The anecdotes on these two pages are culled from A Pope Laughs, *a book to be published in October by Holt, Rinehart and Winston.*

The offices of the Papal Secretary of State are on the ground floor of the Vatican palace, whereas the papal apartments are on the third floor. Cardinal Domenico Tardini, who was John XXIII's first Secretary of State, had worked for many years under Pius XII and found it difficult to get used to the new regime. Whenever John sent for him, he was apt to say, "The one up there is calling me again, just when I have so much to do." Apparently this was reported to John, for one day, after an important conversation on church policy, John took his Secretary of State aside. "*Caro* Tardini," he said, "I should like to straighten you out on one point. 'The one up there' is the Lord of all of us, the eternal Father in heaven. I am merely 'the one on the third floor.' " There was a pause, then a final thrust: "Please, I beg you not to keep throwing confusion in the ranks!"

Angelo Roncalli came from a modest home and had a deep distaste for pomp. Only on really ceremonial occasions did he make use of the *sedia gestatoria,* the papal sedan chair. The *sediari,* the twelve men in scarlet silk and velvet who carry the chair, were called upon far less frequently by John XXIII than by Pius XII. John often went to St. Peter's on foot.

Constantly concerned about the welfare of others, it was inevitable that he would one day ask the *sediari* about their wages and promise them a raise. The papal court was dumbfounded, for this sort of interest in Vatican affairs had not been customary in the previous pontificate. "Why does the Holy Father concern himself with such a trifle?" he was asked by a subordinate. John looked at the man, then stared into the distance for a moment, perhaps envisioning the ethereal figure of his predecessor. Then he replied, "They should receive a bonus to compensate them for the increase in papal weight."

Because of an ancient regulation, the papal apartments were watched over all night by two guards who marched back and forth carrying heavy sabres and wearing high boots with clanking spurs. John XXIII not only considered this procedure an expensive form of display, but found the noise the guards made disturbing. One night, as he was working late at his desk, his annoyance at the sound of measured strides outside the door was

intensified by the coughing of one of the men. Just as the two guards greeted each other at a halt, the Pope opened the door. Both men began to snap out their reports, according to regulations. "Gently, gently," said the Pope, calming them down. "You don't need to get so excited. It would be better for you both to be home in bed. Better to go to sleep. You don't need to watch over me. I am protected by the Holy Spirit."

The guards obeyed promptly, turning around to leave. But the Pope called them back and pressed a little box into the hand of the man nearer to him: "And here are a few pills for your cough. Good night!"

During the first months of his pontificate, John was obliged to give some time to posing for portrait photographers. Bishop Fulton J. Sheen reports that he arrived for an audience just as John had finished one of these sessions. John greeted his visitor with the remark, "The good God has known for seventy-seven years that I would become Pope. Couldn't He have made me a little bit more photogenic?"

Like most people who have to wear glasses for reading and writing, John frequently mislaid his—so frequently that his secretary, his bodyguard, and the Master of Ceremonies all carried an extra pair of glasses in case of emergency. During the solemn opening of the Second Vatican Council in St. Peter's Basilica, the Pope once again could not find his glasses. After searching unsuccessfully in his robes, he said, with a short sigh, "If your eyesight fails, there's nothing you can do about it. That is *God's* will. But misplacing my glasses—that's sloppiness on *my* part."

A worthy Augustinian father used to serve the Pope too assiduously when he offered Mass in his private chapel. It bothered John a little to be assisted so devotedly by this man, and one morning he explained his feeling to the eager helper. "Beginning tomorrow, please assist me just as simply as you would any other celebrant. And if any high official reproaches you, just say, 'I and the Pope have agreed on it.' "

When Roncalli was in France as Apostolic Delegate, he met the Chief Rabbi of Paris and used the occasion to show him his respect. It was at a diplomatic reception which included the heads of all the different religious communities in Paris. The two had a long conversation and discovered that they had many things in common, especially in terms of their human sympathies. When dinner was announced, they found themselves—still talking with great interest and animation—standing side by side in front of the entrance to the dining hall. Nuncio Roncalli did not permit the game of "After you; no, after you" to drag on. He gently steered the Chief Rabbi before him, saying, "The Old Testament before the New!"

John was asked one day by a visitor, "Holy Father, how many men work in the Vatican?" "Half of them," said His Holiness.

A newly appointed bishop, received by the Pope in a private audience, complained that the burden of his new office prevented him from sleeping. "Oh," said John kindly, "the very same thing happened to me in the first few weeks of my pontificate, but then one day my guardian angel appeared to me in a daydream and whispered, 'Giovanni, don't take yourself so seriously.' And ever since then I've been able to sleep."

At a reception in the presidential palace in Paris, Nuncio Roncalli was placed on the left of the Russian Ambassador. While the President greeted his diplomatic guests, the Ambassador whispered mischievously to the Nuncio: "Well, does this mean that even the Vatican is taking a leftist position?" The Nuncio replied quickly with a broad smile: "Yes, they've placed me on the left here so that I can move you all over to the right—I mean, of course, onto the right path!"

"I came from a poor family . . ." was often the way John opened a conversation. Mindful of the tradition of the Church, which pays no attention to a man's origins when it advances him in the priesthood, Pope Roncalli always stressed the equality of men before God. There was no resentment in his voice when he said that his own parents were small winegrowers.

In a private audience with the Pope a politician once complained that the election his party had just lost would bring about his ruin. "No, no," the Pope said encouragingly, "don't be discouraged by your opponent's success. There are always ups and downs in politics. There are only three ways a man can be ruined: women, gambling, and farming. My father chose the most boring of the three."

On March 7, 1963, for the first time in history, a member of the Supreme Soviet paid his respects to the Pope. Alexei Adzhubei, editor of *Izvestia*, and his wife, the daughter of Premier Khrush-chev, were received first in a small audience consisting of Soviet diplomats and foreign correspondents, and then alone, except for an interpreter. Before saying farewell, John gave his blessing with a gesture of inimitable kindness. In a disarming voice he said: "That was only a little blessing. Such a little one can't hurt. Receive it as it was intended—and all your relatives at home were included—in a spirit of reconciliation and for the good of your souls. May peace and justice be always with you."

To receive the first lady of the United States, Pope John wanted to memorize at least enough English for his opening remarks. The Secretary of State, Cardinal Cicognani, drawing on the experience gained during his years of service in Washington, explained to the Pope that she should be addressed as "Madam" or "Mrs. Kennedy." John made use of the few minutes before the wife of the American President entered his private library to practice a few times, "Madam, Mrs. Kennedy, Madam . . ." But the minute she crossed the threshhold, he forgot what he had learned, in joy at her arrival. He went toward her with arms outstretched and cried out, "Jacqueline!"

A well-dressed German priest who came from a diocese of millionaires was telling the Pope how he persuaded his parishioners to contribute to the Church. He said that he was never satisfied with small offerings at Mass. "Before the collection I always say, 'When the basket goes around, I don't want to hear any clinking, only rustling!'"

"Really," John interrupted dubiously, "but isn't that a little —crude?"

"Certainly not, Holy Father," replied the priest eagerly. "My little flock finds the reminder very humorous and a definite stimulant."

John shook his head several times after this explanation. "Do you know, dear friend," he said finally, "that when a poor man *sacrifices* a coin of his, a part of his heart goes into the collection basket with it? That's the reason I would rather hear—clinking."

A Pope has rarely had as little as did John XXIII in the way of material goods to leave behind him. Earlier, he had put together a sum large enough to enable his family to buy back the house in which he and his brothers were born. He left his pectoral cross to Cardinal König, Archbishop of Vienna, who wears it only on special occasions. The Roman physician Piero Mazzoni, who cared for John until the end—staying by him day and night—learned from the dying man that a fountain pen was his only tangible possession. "Take it as a sign of my esteem," whispered John to the doctor. "You have done so much for me, and I have nothing here to repay you for all your care and devotion. I have only this pen. Please take it. It's almost new. I've hardly used it."

Home
Is
What
You
Make
It

Architecture, the mother of the arts, is, like most things parental, considered by her offspring to be a little too sedately planted on the ground—well bred and formalistic, slow to accept new ideas, quick to cater to comfort and convenience. In short, so the argument goes, it does not have enough fun. That folk architecture has never enjoyed the popularity of folk art as a means of self-expression would seem to prove the point. A simple man may indulge in daydreams worthy of a Pharaoh, but when it comes to the hod-and-hammer labors of building for himself, he promptly drops back to earth.

Still, there are mavericks like the three architects whose creations are shown in these pages—true *amateurs* unspoiled by formal training, unfettered by the discipline of structural engineering, and disinterested in practicality for its own sake. Unlike the occasional wishful thinking of professional architects, each of our nonconformists had a dream so insistent, so vivid, that no amount of public disapproval and no appeal to logic could dissuade him from giving it substance.

Modest careers appear to be the common denominator of these Walter Mittys. They have led the kind of lives least likely to provide inspiration—as postman, semi-skilled laborer, handy man—working at night and on weekends at their avocations like "elves . . . whose pastime is to make midnight mushrooms." Each began his monumental task in his forties, as though preparing for immortality, and each has given half a lifetime to its completion. Modest circumstances have forced them to create their architectural phantasmagorias out of the castoffs of Nature and the rest of society: junk, sea shells, broken bottles, scrap metal, chipped crockery, splintered furniture, pebbles, shattered mirrors—all held together with cement, and perhaps a touch of magic.

Ingenuity and intuition have often made these nonprofessionals better engineers than one would expect; in 1959 a committee of Los Angeles citizens, battling condemnation proceedings against the celebrated 100-foot-high Rodia towers in Watts (see overleaf), could confidently call in structural engineers to attest to the towers' stability. In France, too, where the architectural extravaganza opposite was completed in 1902, sentiments have changed from ridicule to awesome respect—even from such an eminent practitioner as Le Corbusier. Today this work of an anonymous civil servant has some status within the sophisticated profession it naïvely burlesques. W.B.

Ferdinand Cheval traveled widely, though he never left the well-worn paths of a French postman. Inspired with a taste for the bizarre and an imagination that knew no bounds, at the age of 43 he began his self-appointed task of achieving "the rebirth of all the ancient architectures of primitive times" in a "Palais Idéal." Where he found precedents for his tombs, grottoes, caryatids, and turrets is uncertain, but most of the materials were gathered on his daily 18-mile rounds in southeastern France. Thirty-four years or, by his estimate, 65,000 hours later, he had finished his grand but uninhabitable 85-foot-long palace. Cheval could proudly say of himself, "The child arrives in this life with hands full of the future. If he knows how to use it, he will leave them filled with remembrances."

ERNIE STOUT

*Simon Rodia, a man of few words but
eloquent purpose, justified 33 years
of labor on his labyrinthine towers
with the simple logic of a child: "I wanted
to do something for the United States
because there are nice people in this country."
Rodia came to Los Angeles from Italy,
prospered as a tile-setter, and in 1921,
at the age of 41, began his grand ex-
voto to America. Using only hand tools (see
their imprints in the panel below),
shells, glass, and such improbables as corn-
cobs, he spun cobwebs of brilliant fantasy.*

PHOTOGRAPHS SEYMOUR ROSEN

At 66, Clarence Schmidt may well be the most embattled artist in America. At least there is no doubt about the spirited warfare currently being waged by his Woodstock, New York, neighbors against his "hazardous" environmental sculpture. Schmidt is by trade an occasional handy man, by avocation a self-styled sculptor-builder. He has spent 44 years embellishing and enlarging what is, by the latest count, a 30-room, four-level pleasure dome. With asphalt as stickum and an inventory that would enrich several junk yards, he continues to erect what some admirers are lately lauding as avant-garde assemblage. Less sanguine townsmen consider their new tourist attraction a sub-versive threat to property values.

The Pepsi-Cola tower at the New York
World's Fair, a sophisticated design from
the studios of Walt Disney, is a rare
example of architectural daydreaming gone
legitimate. Part Pop Art mobile,
part Brobdingnagian tinker toy, this
unconventional windmill is an
adversary worthy of a modern Don Quixote.